Quarterly Review of

EDITED BY T. & R. WEISS

Literature

Poetry Book Series
VOLUME XXXVI

YANNIS PATILIS
Camel of Darkness,
Selected Poems (1970-1990)
Translated from the Greek
by Stathis Gourgouris

WARREN CARRIER
An Ordinary Man

CHRISTOPHER BURSK
The One True Religion

JOSEPH POWELL
Getting Here

FADHIL AL-AZZAWI
In Every Well a Joseph is Weeping
Translated from the Arabic
by Khaled Mattawa

26 HASLET AVENUE, PRINCETON, NEW JERSEY 08540

ACKNOWLEDGEMENTS

WARREN CARRIER: Grateful acknowledgment is made to the editors of *Bare Foot Review* for "The Wind from Cancun" ("While I Sit in My Patio"). *The Formalist* for "After Pindar." *Harvard Magazine* for "Winter" and "Fall" ("The Impetus"). *Northeast* for "View from the Top" and "To Robert Orth, Burma, 1944." *Ohio Review* for "On the River." *Pacific Coast Journal* for "Sailing." *Paisano* (The Maverick Press) for "Rainbow" ("The Cast"). *Quarterly Review of Literature Fiftieth Anniversary Anthology* for "Island," "Sleep," "Desert Places," "Driving North," "An Artist in Winter," "Foxed" ("The Old Guy"), "Letter to Nobody," "The House," and "Stone Creek." *Santa Fe Sun* for "Tree in the Window." *Voices International* for "Jack of All Trades" ("Music in the Night"). *Wallace Stevens Journal* for "Islamorada." *Zanadu* for "Urban Skater."

CHRIS BURSK: Poems in *The One True Religion* have appeared in *Chelsea, Doubletake, Manhattan Review, North American Review, The Sun, New England Review*. Many of these poems were written under a fellowship from the Pew Foundation and during residencies at the MacDowell Colony, Yaddo, and the Virginia Center for Creative Arts, to whom the author owes great gratitude. The author also is grateful to the Vermont College and Warren Wilson MFA programs in Creative Writing. Most importantly the author acknowledges his debt to Interfaith Housing Development Corporation and Libertae, two organizations committed to recovery for those struggling in poverty and in addiction; the award money for *One True Religion* has been donated to them in repayment of this debt.

YIANNIS PATILIS has published eight volumes of poetry: *The Little Guy and the Beast* (1970), *But Now Be Careful . . .* (1973), *In Favor of Fruition* (1977), *Tokens* (1980), *Nonsmoker in the Land of Smokers* [Collected Poems] (1982), *Warm Midday* (1984), *The Scribe's Mirror* (1989), *Voyages in the Same City* [Collected Poems] (1994). The second section of the volume printed here includes an arrangement agreed upon with the poet himself. It is a selection from *The Scribe's Mirror* and the earlier collections. Poems that are individually dated were individually dated in the original volume.

JOSEPH POWELL: I would like to thank the editors of the following magazines in which many of these poems were previously published: *Calapooya Collage, California State Poetry Quarterly, Dickinson Review, Jeopardy, Poetry, The Sucharnochee Review, Trestle Creek, Washington English Journal, Wilderness*. A special thanks to Mark Halperin, Judith Kleck, and Ed Stover for their assistance with this manuscript.

Assistants: Steven Nardi, Bill Davis, Christopher Rovee Karen Emmerich, Tyler Doggett, Jonathan Foer

Designer: Mahlon Lovett

Cover Monotype: Roselyn Karol Ablow, *The Bowl Has Been Abstracted*, Mixed Media, Montage and Collage, 14.5" x 16.5"

YIANNIS PATILIS

Camel of Darkness

Selected Poems (1970-1990)

*Translated
from the Greek
by Stathis Gourgouris*

YIANNIS PATILIS was born in Athens in 1947. A graduate of the Law and the Philosophy School at the University of Athens, he lives in Athens and teaches literature in secondary education. One of the eminent poets of his generation, since the beginning of the 1980s he has also been a significant critical voice on Greek letters. Between 1983-85, he was the co-founder and co-editor of the poetry and music journal *Nesos Island* and of the critical journal *Kritike kai Keimena* (*Critique and Texts*). Since 1986, he has been the editor and publisher of *Planodion*, a journal of literature and the politics of culture. His work has been translated into many languages.

STATHIS GOURGOURIS is Assistant Professor of Comparative Literature and Hellenic Studies at Princeton University. His third book of poems was published in Athens in 1993 and *Dream Nation: Enlightenment, Colonization, and the Institution of Modern Greece* was recently published by Stanford University Press.

CONTENTS

FROM THE SCRIBE'S MIRROR (1989)
AND EARLIER POEMS (1970–1980)

WARM MIDDAY (1984)

I LIVE, therefore I write.
Call them verses.
Call them little goodbyes to life
In the prospect
Of death.

* * *

HOT afternoon,
You make sure it goes unnoticed,
All that without you
Would be startling.
I passed right by it. I left. I travelled.
I went far within the city itself.
I withdrew from what I longed to come across,
Wrapped in the brown cloak of the chemical cloud
With my mind full of cool flesh
Willing to understand nothing.
It is distance that brings about encounters.
And humans always love
What they understand least.
Because what they do understand
Is less than human
And not worth their love.

* * *

I DON'T see why I should leave.
To go where?
Where will I find so many ruins?
So many pieces of the whole?
It's better here.
In the midst of yesterday's ruins
And of the ruins to come.
Alone. In these empty streets.
Just any one man
Strolling along
Stumbling
Facing
The blissful light of the sun.
The grim light.

* * *

THINGS governed
By air and by light.
Rooted in light.
Yet fluid
In their warm senses.
In their silence.
I hang my ear on a clothespin.
The midday muse strolls by
In the soft breeze.
Around me, vacant chairs
And the newspapers swing lightly
On the kiosk's string.
Governments govern no longer.
The light governs
And the five senses.
Sweet madness that governs
The mind.

* * *

I DON'T know the world
Before its fall.
I only know the fall.
So, daily I celebrate it,
Especially during the vast
And glaring afternoons
When I sit in empty squares
And caress with my eyes
These broken pieces.
The most palpable evidence
Of my life.
(Since life is precisely
What breaks to pieces.)

*　*　*

O ATTIC earth,
I love your apartment buildings
　　more than your Parthenon.
Without them I would have never seen you.
White warm columns of tears.
I am in love.
And this
Has no meaning.
And I am happy
For the failure of all meanings.
And I am unprepared
Deeply unprepared for all.

*　*　*

I THOUGHT it over
Next to that broken marble
Besieged by apartment buildings.
A few trees, a couple of flowerpots
A small railing.
The light fell slanted
On the pharmacy's glass.
No, I must not mix
My daily abstractions
With non-existence.
I had thought it over before,
Watching the green waters
Of Erymanthos.
I am thinking of it now
Eyeing the pharmacy's
Red cross
In this deserted square
Next to the marble that whispers:
Leave things alone!
Whatever is broken
Endures longer.

* * *

O ATTIC afternoons!
Large casks of light
White stones.
You left me with little
The least of things.
There is no fear
Harmony only.
The twisted life
Was solved.

In two simple lines.
A belt was undone.
The handsome buildings
The awnings
The shiny cars.
Here and there a bit of green
In midair, so I can't step on it.
A small still cloud.
And mountains,
Great petrified winds
Surrounding the Attic buildings.
There! Everything resolved itself.
In so much light
That all of it together makes
One lucid darkness.

Yes! I work noon-hours.
Supervisor.
I oversee the light
The sky, the apartment buildings.
So that nothing diminishes.
So many buildings, so many people.
So many bodies, wounds. So many cigarettes.
So much grief.
All of you end in light.
For light itself
Shall be in my care.
And when I die
Someone else shall
Take my place.

* * *

I AM in light. I am not the light.
A brief match
In the face of a vast sun.
With thought entire
I adulterate feelings.
But I also think
In favor of feelings
(When I submit to the alleys
Of vision.)
I live in air.
In light.
Sometimes, I turn the light off
And breathe in darkness.
(Rehearsals
To get used to Hades.)

* * *

I HAVE NOTHING against the heat.
It favors solitude. Clears out the streets
Liberates the cool ranges
Of thought.
My footsteps bring me to a bookstore.
Yes, I am cultured!
The books on the window are my witness.
But do I exist?
I remember titles, names, footnotes.
And I am young. And there's still much to learn.
Yet, the problem
Remains.
Should I perhaps turn the hourglass?
And if I don't,
Time will.
When they will flow into nothing,

Titles, names, footnotes.
When my identity finally falls away.
My most respectable address
And my name.
Just then,
When they will pin it all
On my lapels and pockets
For the police officials
To bring me home
When I t r u l y begin
To exist.

* * *

I EXIST to rob non-existence.
From there, I strive to bring back
Marvelous poems.
Transparent, brilliant, ineffable.
But on the way they drop from my hands; they break.
I patch them up. I glue them with words.
Human words.
With what I know, and see, and hear.
And I ruin them with what exists.

* * *

I DON'T know how I found myself in the center.
I trusted the newspapers, the radio.
The interminable march of vehicles.
But again I was wrong.
Because no center existed, no limit.
What exists belongs only to the margins.
The center occupies eternal non-existence.

* * *

FLAMING Hippocrates St.
Without a breath, deserted
As if from a neutron bomb.
Not even a drop of spit in my mouth.
Nor sweat making the trousers stick.
I gaze ahead at electronic traces.
How they shine, wrapped
In their coolest darkness!
Fountains of sounds reaching me here.
Spraying me all over
Like a little dry tree next to the gutter.

* * *

YOU DON'T know what you're doing.
You mature in the most vulgar perfection
Committing a crime
Against the average.
You are much beyond whichever "I love you"
And an elementary sense of intellect

Does not allow me to speak
Of breasts and thighs.
You don't know what you're doing.
Even if they read you this poem
You would understand nothing.
You are still pure.
You get on buses and live with girlfriends.
You, an unconscious land-mine
Waiting unbeknownst
For the one who'll descend on it.

* * *

THE DEEPER I hide you within me
The more beautiful you emerge.
I think my eyes make you beautiful.
But how literary!
Nothingness makes you beautiful.
In time you will succumb

To the particulars.

* * *

EROS, red does not suit you.
Touch suits you. And sight, above all.
But, Eros, to whom does sight belong?
You tie an eye on the *outside* and shield from us
Who is the one who sees.

* * *

AND WHAT IF, EROS, *inside* does not exist?
If all there is *inside* is spleens and livers,
Organs and circulations?
Why shouldn't I, Eros, become a wolf?
To howl and kill and violate.
Why do I sit upon this hill
And gaze at birds and rooftops
When inside all those apartments
Bodies without *inside* long
To howl, to be violated, to be killed?

* * *

WHY DO I BOTHER thinking?
Better to go along without thought.
When I think I fall, and what
Compulsion from an idiot
Who thought he was
                because he thought!
How beautiful, my feet touching
The sidewalk.
How warm, the sidewalk.
What air
                what thoughtless blue!
There, my one foot follows the other.
And from my eye slide softly
Faces—arms
                trees—windows.
Why do I need the total picture?
How total and how
                totalitarian?
Ah, my sweetest shattering
My afternoon.
The fountain.

* * *

AH GIRLS
I am your thief
Whom time
Shall crucify.

* * *

WHAT ARE YOU, a bicycle?
Is it question or response?
Are you asking the world or answering it?
You stand there untouched.
And yet, nothing untouched
Is part of this world.
Unless we exempt the world entire.
Therefore, nothing.
Just polished provocation.
But look at me.
Smoking a cigarette
Behind the glass.
My tired shoulders
The beard.
How useless,
        How used
                How recycled.

* * *

AND YOU, my shoes,
I put you on, I take you off.
You must think I can't make up my mind.
But you don't know about sleep or love.
What it means for the sun to set
And to rise.
What it means to lie naked
With another's nakedness.

* * *

I LOOK at our clothes
Thrown quickly on the floor
Before our lovemaking.
What a mess! All of them mixed together
Like the clothes of those unlucky ones
Who were stood against the wall
Or packed into the gas chambers.
How lucky we are.
We'll separate them with our hands.
We'll slip them on our bodies and leave.
Even if we never meet again.

* * *

I LOVE humans.
Their warm bodies.
Not what humans see.
In the roaring marketplace.
Leaves Wind Death.

Nothing-names.
What I see.
In order to live.
To be.
No need for anyone else
To see me.
It's enough
That light itself does.

* * *

I SIT at Café Eternal Dark
And stare outside at the light.
It's free.
A treat from the nothing inside.

* * *

HOW vast an anonymity death is.
(And what Memory,
My God!
It forgets
N o o n e !)

* * *

HOW vast an antonym death is.
Jesus gave us the name of salvation
John, Elizabeth, Charalambos.
But *He* removes the names.
Unstitches bodies
Along with some naive headstones.
What a vast monument death is.
How uncracked-unreturnable.
Uncracked? And unreturnable?
With an old man's despair
I abandon myself, Christ, to your memory.

* * *

NO TO THE GREAT fetishes.
Socialism, Revolution, Freedom.
Nothing that's written in capitals.
For me, it's enough
A breast in small letters.

* * *

OF ALL THE WORDS I meet
I watch for the most beautiful,
The most slender, most firm
Most young.
I imagine them nude, literal.
Without adjectives and nonsense.
I wait for them in late afternoon.
When they return

Carefree and all alone.
And I fall on them there,
At the apartment's entrance
Or by the newstand.
When they feel a tug at their hair
Their eyes light up like stars.
They never shout or weep.
Because at heart they also long
To be attacked.
They yearn to lie down
In the poem.

* * *

HEAT brought the west wind.
It came by night and whirled up
Leaves of pistachio and olive.
How this wind put my thoughts
In order!
Walking down Polytechnic St.
The "Odyssey" was closing at "Three Stars".
Someone played Polyphemos, the drunkard.
Out of his mouth dribbled wine
And bits of men—
Nearby someone was laughing.
Others revving their motorcycles.
And you, my destitute Muse,
      sharing with me your whispers,
The world was always verse.

* * *

THAT SAME NIGHT with the wind blowing
I sat on the bench in the lonesome square
Recalling myself.
It was definitely me:
As if I held a photograph in my hands.
I was a day emptied of its light.
A rumor I had just learned about me.
The science tormenting me in the day
Was finished. Now
Only the body remembered. Its scant light
Windblown all over the flagstones.
In my hands I held a few voices.

* * *

LET'S PLANT mulberry trees,
You tell the kids in class.
Their leaves work like filters.
You tell them of the bomb.
How only thick bricks will remain.
(Many will still manage to get away,
I thought sarcastically.)
Don't be upset, Virginia.
None of us will die.
The beautiful will rise.
The ugly ones will fall.
The same in the next round.
Until they come across a bit of beauty
And rise a little.

* * *

EROS
You're nothing but
The ignorance
Of him who longs.
I fell ill.
I came to know ignorance
And now I long for you.
Even in daylight
I found no sleep.
Of all creatures
Only you—
And some drugstores—
Stay up all night.
But for you, Eros
I found
No drug.

* * *

O NOW, I WANT TO DRINK a glass of light
From this hot afternoon
Dusty, infected, and forgotten.
Because even this injured light
Will slowly dry up.
And I shall then become a camel of the darkness.
For I must hold out the long nights,
Nights when pill-maniacs roam the streets.

* * *

WHICH should I choose?
The light of the sun or the light of love.
The one shows you the great waves.
The other helps you get lost in them.

* * *

WHY should I write these poems?
Why not walk to the newspaper stand,
Or gaze at the flowerpots on the window,
Or drink some water?

Why not leave my self
In this chair,
   Forgotten
     And unjudged?

FROM THE SCRIBE'S MIRROR (1989)
AND EARLIER POEMS (1970-1980)

ARGO

For just a pack of cigarettes
An afternoon beer outside Orchomenos
A dusty sunset between two buses,
I'll do whatever you demand, dear Reader
The Wandering Rocks and Sirens are mere routine
The summary of Orpheus, a midnight bar like a dogpound
Scylla and Charybdis, sheer tedium
And Polydeuces, just a suburban karate school
But this fatigue, like any other working man's
Departing twice a month from Colchis
Caressing small *Golden Fleece* souvenirs,
I shall remain where you left me last
Temporarily exhausted between two more feats
As if among the furniture of an exhausted move
All but your chair whose loss, of course,
You no longer have cause to fear
As you once did, remember?
When uninvited you suddenly saw me in your room
Avenger
With a blackened stare, one-sandaled vagabond.

Summer 1989

ARGOS

O Argos
Empire of loneliness
A man arrives at your gate
A double Teiresias
No one seems to pay attention
As he rides his bicycle
In-between speaking bipeds
The human bodies

With brains of swine
They eat pizzas
And watch football
With Galileo's glasses
They don't perceive
The slippery streets
The permanent carelessness
Of death

He an old man child
Can hear the silence
Read the unwritten
See the invisible
He carefully scans the names
On the doorbells
Tantaliades, Atreidopouloi, Pelopides
Owners of wheels
Creators of garbage
The leisure men of Argos.

A SOLDIER'S DREAM IN AN
APARTMENT AT PATISSIA

I dreamt I was defending Thermopylae with Leonidas.
It was Sunday, and we were drying our hair out in the sun.
Suddenly, the Persians arrive with Ephialtes.
They demand a peaceful passage to Athens.
Things get out of hand. The seers look to the satellites
    for advice screaming, "We took it! We took it!"
Bomber planes cover the sun with arrows.
Leonidas reminds us of Leonidas and his three hundred.
"Greeks fight better in the shade," he shouts
    as he runs away.
"Greeks fight better against Greeks."

RETURN TO THE ACROPOLIS

A tubercular coffee-delivery man races up and
    down the 8th floor
driven by an unconquerable survival instinct,
holding in midair coffees propelled by legal papers.
In the elevator he becomes a terrorist to himself.
In the mirror he faces an innocent hostage,
a peace-loving man with an apron of white
    pendelic marble.

THE NEW LIFE

A rock becomes an issue of demonology.
It becomes the stone of humanity's trials.
It stands at the end of each act sending you back
    to the beginning.
Everyone gathered shouting outside the rock's home,
when a handsome youth with canvas shoes showed up
    at the door:
"I came to banish the regime of the rock," he said to the
    fatigued crowd,
"to substitute the unbuilt light for the petrified."
The people sighed with relief
and withdrew to nearby hills for a smoke.

KING KONG

He is King Kong, the patron saint of civil servants.
When the civil servant sees this monstrous body
emerging from behind buildings,
he brims with a secret agony.
He stands up baffled, as if to sharpen his pencil,
or searches through drawers, feigning indifference,
while casting tender glances at the window.
Yes, the State Machine does pose something threatening,
    something colossal,
but it lacks the monstrous rush of the supernatural.
When the civil servant goes on strike or makes love,
it's the cry of King Kong tearing through his chest.

MAN IS A DOG

All of humanity's pains become dogs.
When a man speaks softly in his living room,
his pain is hidden in the heart of a dog
    who aches to leap down the stairs,
      out into the street,
and fall howling under the wheels of a truck.

INTERNALLY AND EXTERNALLY

Internally we belong to the sky
Externally we live in Korydallos
Internally we walk on water
Externally we are classified submarines
Internally we are crucified on the middle cross
Externally we tear at our garments.

Internally we confess externally
Externally we repent internally
Internally and in part externally

Externally with motor-scooters
Internally with angels' wings
Intimidating basketball stars externally
Five feet tall internally
Internal conviction, external phenomena
Internally apparent, externally bound
Freelyinsane internallyexternally

Natives of the Himalayas externally
Internally *the Himalayas themselves.*

POST(MORTEM)MODERN

When they heard
Now or Never,
They all cried *Never,*
And lowered their heads
Over their work
Again.

A BODY IN THE APARTMENT

(souvenir of a decade)

I.

Sometimes it happens that a gust of wind
A humble servant of church bells
Passionately swoops down from the mountain's shadow
To bring you—now—a message baptized
In silence and dream
Sometimes it happens that you lie down waiting
As if the rear-guard of the future
And calm as if after a burial
This gust of wind
Passing through the interstices of men
To reach your door.

It was an evening
Like the one when the *chiding* Archilochos
Confronted Thasos from afar, grunting
There she is, like the backbone of an ass
Weighed down with savage wood—
That kind of evening
When the first time it was seen in London
Everyone started flying at once
The moment when the psalm sprouted in my mouth
Like a seed of wheat that grows
Until it turns to wholesome bread.

II.

During those same years
There were some people who fried eggs
There were others who were enlightened
I remember someone who inhabited a hand
A palm he called the Grace of God.

And there was an old man who sang
As long as the song lasted he grew young again
And then got smaller and smaller
Until he became an infant wailing
And his mother would come and take him
Take him up to the sky.

During those same years
Someone was extracting uranium from garbage
One night he had lost his faith while flying
Finding himself in a trash-can
A real war raged all around
They sprayed him from above with black cards
While his own people were flying inside caskets.

III.

Sometimes it happens that a gust of wind
A tomb digging in your memory
Scatters the dust all over your papers
Right then you want to hold on to something
You want to hold on to the white wall
To the cypress tree.

It's raining
Inside cafés, inside homes
You want to stay
You're holding on to the rain
You're holding on to the cypress tree

And yet,
You must be *violated* and you must *violate*
And above all you must die
You must become dust before you become sky.

IV.

Nothing is more certain, the sky gave you birth
Here is your body
The living relay-staff of so many people's love
You can see their grief
On Attic epitaphs
Or engraved on roof-tiles
Just before the fall of Sirmion or Viminakion.

Perhaps because of those long-haired Avars
This body, passing from hand to hand,
Found its way to this apartment
Because this body is the bread
Eaten and never spent
It is Socrates' numbness after the hemlock
The severed tongue and arm
Of Maximus, the Confessor.

This body
Whose only weapon is its nakedness
Was hunted by the all-mighty, the all-armed
The emperors, the vlads, the czars, the commissars
Its beautiful flesh was hunted
By fleshless ideas.

V.

Not those with pseudonyms
Nor those who drop leaflets
From the clouds

Here is my body—
History's living fountain.

(1980)

THE LAMP

On days we were enveloped
By the cloud
The song would come
From the engine-room:

The earth sprouts
New seed
From the cabin of punishment
The trumpet's mouth
Revives
The exhausted ones.

There is something
That renews the world
In its moment of burial.
A shroud unwrapped
By ignorance.
The coded messages of the birds
On the terraces of trees.

The funereal Priapus!

Something inscribed
In the light
    Of a grape.

The times are all upside down, and yet
As water in a sinking
      ship
Beauty pours in from everywhere
The verses
Few crumbs on the paper
Can feed the tired ones
      the hungry ones
Can tear through mountains
      cross over the sea
Fall from the sky
      on raised glasses
      on tender flesh
Our heart sticks out
Like a rabbit's ears
Behind the fern
The gunshots give it birth
Indifference feeds it
The ice keeps it warm
Soft and red
The patrons of melancholy grow, and yet
The song never stops.

POETIC THEORY

The poem
Is built
Where there was
Nothing
To symbolize
The Nothing
That was
In its place

THE DEAD AT THE CLOCK IN KYRRISTOS

I'll think good thoughts for them
Entrust them to the angel with the white hands
And to the other who pours thick hale from his shield
And to the one who drinks now from the jug
They wait for me bundled in their ragged coats
Beneath the Elms
Gazing at the naked branches with the raven nests.

They wait for me to pour wine, milk and honey
On their shadows.

A WRITTEN ANSWER TO THE MOUNTAINS

The fortune of a piece of paper thrown in a coat pocket
Each day wanting to change something from the day before
After it scatters everything all over
Like a truck that kills ninety sheep on the national road
    and goes on
It can't be that way, and since it can't be any other way
Each day wants to change something from the day before
Perhaps the fortune of a piece of paper thrown in a coat
    pocket.

BEAUTIFUL LYRE

As to this air
Stones built by the wind
Will this blossom of grain hold out?
Will the corn leaf?
The day passes
With large mirrors of silence on its wings
Over the barren parts of Summer
Sweeps up the few thorns
Caresses those stones
Built by the wind
Moving on
While from high mountains descends
The dark Winter
Demanding identities.

ATTEMPT AGAINST SILENCE

Since the vortex of colours
Is white, is silence
The great contortion of all that's spoken
No one will be able to analyze
Silence, no spectroscope
A desert inside everyone
Thick dust that time's slow wind
Cannot exhaust
Raising the small clouds of idle talk
In various shapes (sometimes poetic)
Which change shape again since
Dust will never settle
Because time—the one who blows—
Is Madness (and nothing
Stops Madness). The fools we are
Continuing to talk of silence
As if a grain of sand could talk
Of the desert
(Which settles inside everyone).

SHADOWS CASTING BODIES

Shadows casting bodies
As the Muse of Woe on Pythia St. says—
You move your lips and they come
Voices from other lips
Shadows casting bodies
On a wall made of paper
Until life becomes four walls.

And yet, you'll never find her there
With her brave metaphors
She is constantly on the move
In vain the new reader would ring
Each time anew the doorbell of reading
While the invitation clearly spelled it out
For poets only
In other words, for those drowned
And not the ones who sought the safety raft
For those naive ex-non-poets
Who sought the body first.

WESTERN CHAIR

He sat on the café's western chair
resembling the little naked table in a field
kissed by the wind cooled by the cloud
washed tightly by the humble cloth.
Fresh air, the mind, a cup of blossoms
gift from the void and the furnace of the sun
as it marches to its ephemeral glory
like Hannibal's stool in the olive-grove centuries.

What was it nearing him that he did not know its cause
he had no dictionary but he had the notion.
His clay eyelids caught the immaterial light!
He remembers ancestors packed in their tent
chased away from their natural cover
for something incomprehensible and arrogant
deprived of the social security of innocence.
He sat on the café's western chair
where darkness gives birth to bread
like the great wheat-fields give birth to Khans.

METAPSYCHOSIS

It's better this way, without power
So many channels, from Palestine
All the way to Ilium and beyond
To Yerivan, Armenia, all those wretched souls
Searching around in ruins, in the cold
Now, ruins I know well
The violence of Thyestis
The terrifying cries of the little boys
The refugee life in Sparta
And that was only the beginning
The other things, the fortunes
Brought me from the unholy hunt
(There's a future for ecology in yesterday)
Which levelled so many homes besides
Not only mine
And all the other fortunes, the wretched Trojans
On the plain
And those severed heads all in a row
On the front pages of hexameters
The poets have said it so much better
See Loeb, 1978
A bilingual edition
Down to this point when my punished
Soul descends at last
(Yet, from something strange forgiven and forgotten)
Into the empty Hades, this apartment
On a cross-street off Patission
Better this way caressing nipples
Small buttons
And switching channels.

BIRDS

The sky cracks in places
Like plaster sometimes in whole pieces
Which lose their luster as they fall
Become opaque, soft, and warm
They grow fur and down and feathers
And on their brown color now
They mirror dirt

This is the sky from up close
This is how it comes closer
Everyone now can reach it
(Even those blessed children
With the sling-shots)
Because it exhausts you high up
Eternal and unfractured
Without love's caresses to wear you down
Something you cannot stand and break
In places, crack and strip in whole pieces
Which lose their luster as they fall
They grow fur and down and feathers
(Because nobody kills you without a motive)
And they fall
             They fall
Upon this earth where constantly the sky
Comes to die.

PERSEPHONE

to Elsa

If only I could get lost
Like all who pick flowers get lost
He thought
Crossing the traffic lights in Omonia
To go down
Not down to Hades (not yet)
But down Omonia's immobile escalators
If only I could become a grain of Spring
Which condescended even
To the dusty tents of Kerameikos St.
He said as he took
A leaflet from a young woman
Calling all textile workers
To one more twenty-four hour strike
If only I had twenty-four hours
Of absolute life
Caressing the vibrant breast
Of this day here
Settled with divine violence
On the eyes
He thought, head down, as he passed
By the wooden flute
Accompanying the tape player
Of a blind man adorned with lottery tickets
If I only had some luck, some light
From that one kind residing inside the other
As I climb the stairs up
To the world above
A virgin child to get lost
Like all who pick flowers got lost
And once again to find myself
Upon the earth.

Spring 1988

PICTURES OF A YOUNG WOMAN

(a selection of almost haikus)

I hold a lily
I've dressed my angel
With dust

*

My eyes took a trip
Over your body
Look, it's dark out

*

Mouthfuls of darkness
In my mouth I shove
Your black hair

*

Feasts of shoulders
Under your arms blossom
Tender mournings

*

Small breast
Feed on my kiss
So you can grow

*

On a divan
A tender galaxy
With black holes

*

44 PATILIS

White moon
Nests in your belly
Take me in

*

You exist so fully
Even imagination itself
Is your own creature

*

Before you, each word
Must keep one minute
Of silence

*

Only the mirror
Endures your sight
Without shattering

*

Even the poet Ritsos
Seeing you naked
Would stop writing

*

Even the wind
Blowing upon you
Became a sculptor

*

Just like the flame
You turn it all to ash
Although you flicker

*

A breast in hand
Longtime before you drink
From a glass again

*

Like a piece of paper
Eros has printed you
On both sides

*

O my mad mouth
See if you can speak now
With two tongues

*

Two bodies were robbing
Each other
They gave up everything

*

I sow mirrors
To nurture
My two mad eyes

*

What do these two want?
Two lunatics wrestling
Inside the mirror

*

Three black flames
Nest in your body
As you sleep

*

Small afternoon
On a small cloud
You have been latched

*

You are asleep
And the moon
Mocks me

*

Come wind
Bring me her voices
From foreign lands

*

Of all your positions
You kept one secret

Absence

Go on, my soul, take to
Your good turns of mind
Like glasses of wine
Each one bringing
The next.

NOTES

1. *I Thought It Over*. page 11,"Erymanthos": A river in the province of Arcadia, Peloponnese. Its clear waters reflect the luscious nature that surrounds it. Known in antiquity as the site of the fourth task of Hercules.

2. *Flaming Hippocrates St.* page 15, "Hippocrates St.": One of the most busy and polluted thorough-fares in downtown Athens. An unhealthy experience.

3.*What Are You, A Bicycle?* page 18, "A bicycle life" is a Greek idiom for an unbearably exhausting and stressful existence.

4. *Argos*. page 27, "The human bodies/with brains of swine": Reversal of Circe's magical act in the *Odyssey* (Book X 239-240).

5. *A Soldier's Dream in an Apartment in Patissia*. page 28, "Patissia": Formerly a bourgeois neighborhood with small private houses and gardens, now a terribly crowded neighborhood with densely packed apartment buildings.

"Ephialtes": According to Herodotus, the man who led the Persians through a mountain path to the rear of Leonidas' army. A euphemism for "traitor to the nation", freely used during the post-Civil War era to describe Greek communists.

"We took it! We took it!": Parody of Leonidas' famous answer to Xerxes at Thermopylae ("Come and take it!").

"Greeks fight better against Greeks": Reference to the Civil War and the general anticommunist ideology that persisted in the Army until 1974.

6. *Internally and Externally*. page 31, "Korydallos": Working class neighborhood in Piraeus, known particularly as the location of large prison quarters.

7. *A Body in the Apartment*. page 32, "Sirmion or Virminakion": Byzantine cities in the Danube region, conquered by the Avars in late 6th century AD.

"Maximus, the Confessor" (580-662 AD): Chief grammarian in the Court of Emperor Heraclius, later turned monk who fought against what he saw as the monothelite heresy, which was at that time tolerated by the Patriarch. The Church ordered his exile and torture and, finally, had his tongue and right arm amputated. Distinguished now as an author of important theological texts.

8. *Metapsychosis*. page 41, The title is a pun on the word "metempsychosis" (reincarnation). The poem's persona is a latter-day (reincarnated? psychotic?) Agamemnon.

9. *Persephone*. page 43, "Omonia": Central square in downtown Athens, site of the old subway's most extensive underground stop.

"Kerameikos St.": A street near Omonia that leads to the cemetery of the ancient city.

AFTERWORD: Poetry's Utopia

One of the reasons I love poetry has to do with the great resistance it poses—relative to other modes of art—to the contemporary means of social assimilation. I am not referring, surely, to the poets themselves but to the nature of the art (*techne*) they practice. First of all, poetry, in its very materiality as a process, hardly lends itself to the aims and purposes of the culture industry. It bears no forgiveness for mass production as is the case with the novel; I do not know of a single poetry book that rests comfortably on the best seller list. The poem on the printed page (which constitutes the exclusive existential space—*topos*—of modern poetry) cannot be videotaped, cannot be tape-recorded, cannot become picture to hang on a wall, cannot be photographed or transcribed into a screenplay. It is poetry's foundation that we see and hear it internally. Poetry, therefore, signifies an art-form that demands less than any other the participation of other material practices in order to be produced and understood. Poetry is content to employ the least refined materials in order to come into being; pencil and paper is simply enough. It is exclusively an art (*techne*) of the spirit, essentially untamable by technology. In its attempt to turn art works into commodities, the culture industry is by necessity bound to seek out technology, a coupling that inevitably produces mass culture.

The resistance to mass culture that poetry poses by its very nature has led in effect to its social marginalization. Even its own mode of consumption is not quite socially determined. I can imagine a specific reading space for almost any sort of book: for the novel, the train or the beach suit it fine; a biography is comfortably read out in the veranda; a volume of essays demands a chair and a desk, while a scientific treatise requires, in addition, a pen for note-taking and a study. It is with great difficulty, however, that I imagine a specific space or a specific bodily posture perfectly suited to the reading of poetry. It seems that there is no such thing.

There is, however, something else that makes the conjunction between poetry and the present global reality even more difficult, and it resides in the intense anti-narrative character of contemporary lyricism. At the moment when the entire planet is transformed via the constant expansion of information science into a global village—in which television, newspapers, technical knowledge, and entertainment organize the human experience according to the rules of a commonly shared global narrative, a planetary serial whose previous episode is known to all and whose anticipated future is subscribed to with anxious curiosity—poetry comes to preserve the fragmentation, the shrapnel, of private experience and to guarantee that human sensibility will continue to remain discontinuous and asymmetrical to the new totality of information.

*

I began writing poetry at the end of the 1960s in Athens. There was a military dictatorship, but the roads of sensitivity were free and open. I discovered poetry by reading the Greek post-War poets. In those days, no one really knew them except those few in the poetry community. I thus learned the crucial lesson: poetry was a personal matter that had no connection to mechanisms of power, to the large public, to publicity. The miracle presented before me was how could a "little thing" like a verse manage to render accurately an elusive feeling or circumscribe with plenitude the meaning of an entire era. Little verses were fashioned then without sound, in haste and in secret, on café tables or inside a bus. It was an ideal art for the pockets of wanderers. The life of poetry collections was just as subterranean. Even though they circulated in unbelievable numbers, they were a species you rarely came across for purchase. If you exempt those collections found in used bookstores, with their pages uncut and their dedications resounding the loud names of the recipients, you could only place your hopes in the postman or in the oftentimes unknown individual next to you at a gathering, who all of a sudden would reach into his bag and pass around large, thin, flat objects, like discs.

I believe that the way one comes to be connected with poetry, either as its reader or its creator (qualities that often coincide in the same person) has something very personal about it, since, as I have already mentioned, poetry is the art-form that safeguards more than any other the private realm. For me, on the other hand, poetry was the art-form that helped me experience, in a deeper spiritual way, whatever is open to the collective experience, whatever is shared and public. The streets of Athens gradually became the realm of a sort of metaphysical experience, in which the Parthenon's broken marbles within the surrounding ashen fog of the Attic basin were transformed from the ideal of immaculate perfection to the symbol of the eternity of deterioration and the enigma of human suffering.

I was born in Colonus in 1947, a lower-class neighborhood near the center of Athens, in the time of the most savage Greek civil war. In the space of the ancient grove and the Platonic Academy we lived, blind men like Oedipus, who in trying to know themselves "totally", gouged their own eyes out. In this same space whose demographics is changing rapidly, a multitude of Moslems now wander about—a small Islam in the heart of Athens, offspring of the great new overturnings of our time. There is nothing paradoxical about the scene. On the contrary, it had been predicted by the old myth: the borders between cultures are not mainly geographical but internal; they belong to the glorious human endeavor of learning oneself and controlling one's fate. But the desire for the absolute "enlightenment" of self and the complete handling of history inheres something totalitarian and self-destructive that inevitably increases global suffering. The civilization of self presupposes this painful realization that tempers the possessive arrogance of knowledge and permits the symbiosis with our stranger (*xenos*) and uncanny (*paraxenos*) Other. If in his dramatic swan-song, Sophocles chose to bring Oedipus (in order to roll back his wretched fate and restore his heroism) to a grove belonging to a hometown hero, the master horseman Colonus— a grove dedicated to those terrible goddesses of justice, the Eumenides, from which the gods would then call Oedipus near—we now know that this call was made possible in the terms of an extraordinary poetry and that the real Colonus, the one which played host to this archetype of tortured humanity, was none other than the poet's profound reverence toward what is human distilled in his iambic trimeters. The poet's reverence was a Colonus of the spirit, always already constituting the inalienable space (*topos*) of poetry.

for Judy and Ethan and Greg
and Malcolm and Marilyn
and Joan and Bill
and Ellen

WARREN CARRIER

An Ordinary Man

An Ordinary Man is WARREN CARRIER'S fifth collection of poetry. He has also published five novels, a book of translations, and has edited three books. He has published numerous poems, articles, stories, translations, and reviews in literary journals, and has recently completed a new novel, *Justice at Christmas*. An emeritus university chancellor and professor of English, he now lives in Galveston, Texas.

CONTENTS

AN ORDINARY MAN

AN ORDINARY MAN

He burrows through the dark. In the thin
glow of morning he attends the querulous crakes.
He interrupts the air to speak your name.
He sits like a cairn in a field to mark his place.
Who looks at him from windows gliding by?
The day is a drum. Its tremors are terrible signals,
ablating the ruptured edges of the sky
until the shambled earth is all there is.

Rats gnaw at rafters, pears go rotten
on the ground. Nature persists in nests and boscs.
Contriving its images is his natural gig
that turn in a day to sawdust and shriveled pits.
His hand is shaky now, but sets them right,
these odd devices that tote him through the night.

URBAN SKATER

A bundled boy, he skated
through sheets of glass.

A hell of mills upwind,
his breath was sulphur and soot.

A drone of obstinate belief
stabbed his infected ears.

No towel-wrapped iron
mothered the pain.

Snared, he glided
into obsidian.

THE BOY IN THE PHOTOGRAPH

His mother's mother and father sit in the middle.
Their sons and husbands of their daughters stand
in back. Their daughters sit beside in a row.
Grandchildren sit crosslegged on the ground—
except for the boy standing at the end,
holding a fuzzy rabbit dead in his arms.
The animal is part of giving thanks
that day. He dreamed a lot when he was young.

He is the faces of the dead, a print
of creatures from these fields, the sea beyond.
The generations hold him in their arms,
this house, these trees, this ritual of fall.
His dreams take singular shots. No one else
can narrate him or polka in his style.

SAILING

He's in a sail plane
without the sail
without wind
floating.
He sees his body
above the wide ground.
He understands everything.

His father is smaller
shrunken from his new perspective.
Once he bulked

a magnitude of flesh
a self of opinions and indulgences
possessing the power to resist.
Now he is something else.

He has never seen his father
from this distance
a body within the limits of his body
that something else contained in it
that other being who
though separate
has always been a part of him
a familiar alien.

They are in the water.
His father hands him the tiller.
The silence is surprising.
Water unfolds from the side of the boat.
An invisible power pushes out the sails
like the cheeks of a horn blower.
Bring her about, his father says.
He moves the tiller too quickly.
The boat rises on its side.
You do it, he says.
You do it, his father says.
The sails crack and the boom flies over their heads.
He is crying. It's all right, his father says.
You did it.

Was it always like that
the awkwardness
the edge of wreckage
the silence that drove him?

All that's left is his name.
And the dates.
Nineteen something or other.
Then nineteen something or other.
Does it matter?
You fill in the rest.

He goes to the book store
where once he met a homely Hindi
who wanted to be a poet.
She isn't there.

He sits on a granite block
near the mole where the cats live.
Dozens of them. A colony of cats.

A poem in his pocket, he tails a homeless loco
pushing the planet in his cart.

I'm on the rocks,
he says to himself.
Less than I was,
more than I shall be.
Old Tom, eating apricots,
mewing by the sea.

HE SAYS:

    List things. Let them speak.
    Put one here
                            one there:
    pear trees in the morning
    moving gently   light
    licking your nipples
    hair sleeting down
                            from crown to bung
                glistening
    plums
            like bruised lips in a basket
    soft bells tinkling down a stalk
                like foxglove
                            aromas
    pekoe
    cinammon
                            hands
    arms   thighs
            floating skydown in the leaves
            in cups
    into rooms where night is hidden
                            onto surfaces
    polished by the sun————
    wherever they can touch.

ISLAND

His island is a fenny spit. Life enters
and leaves the muddy slough under the drag
of the moon. Gulls climb in closing light to scout
for prey. Their cries are his mutilated
shouts to mainlands and distracted friends.
He reaps the plastic and the clumps of crude
the sea lifts and layers on the sand,
the carcasses of bitter weeds, and now
and then a perfect shell, emptied of death
and beautiful. Will he leave such a form
as nature makes? Listeners will hear themselves—
not these dopplered plaints or the scavenger's screak.

DANCING IN THE MORNING

The morning plays its usual pavan.
He dances up and down a cockled tide.
White wimples in the air make a gull—
at the scend of every wave a hunting eye.
The lookers look for images to whistle.
Their notes perform the score the dancer wings.
He sees what he has seen: the sun's ascension,
the rendezvous of bodies limb by limb,
horizons of lost affection and the drowned.
In the sky's transparency, a field of light
beyond his span, he spins to one more round.
He chants: I'll dance all day until at night
I lay me down with images to sleep,
never to wake, and not a thing to keep.

HE SAYS TO THE MAN WALKING HIS DOG:

for Bill Winslade

Stalk the wards where waiting is blind man's bluff
(yes or no among the almost bodies),
or jog the detritus along the Gulf
where your dog bounds in and out of water,
shagging gulls.
                    They fly away, those raucous
souls, unplugged from their salty islands.
Neither just nor evil, your dog noses
a broken wing, then runs on for the live ones.
That's the game, my friend. No is nil,
foolish spit in the eye of a quirky wind.

AFTER PINDAR

The felled oak feeds a winter fire
Its momentary flame. No bird will rise
To sign another season from these limbs,
A roof he cut pitched to bitter winds,
Beams that stood no longer than their source.
This is a tale to tell us what to know:
There's nothing left in the place he came from now,
Nor will there be in any place he goes.

WISCONSIN

A year stops. Who scuds in the kick of the wind?
No ordinary man is left to know.
Farms of stubble bed rivers of rippled snow.
Wisconsin winter, what else is there to find?
Maples go bald and stiffen to the bone.
Since Wisconsin, many years have passed,
precipitates of a past beyond his past.
This no of north is practice for the cold.
And this is how it settles: in ice and ache,
corn stalks askitter beside a frozen lake.

ADIOS

for Bill Stafford

You go.
He stays, for awhile.
This is a piece of work,
not a blossoming hawthorne bush
or a winter oak
or the rocky bed of a creek under ice.

You go, like a leaf
cleft from sap,
falling and floating downwater.

He stays, a leaf,
reddened, rusted,
sucking the last life,
waiting for wind.

What is left is a piece of work,
durable for a time.
A sound in the ear,
deer tracks in mud,
slate, uncovered in another life,
mysterious, perhaps beautiful.

TREE IN THE WINDOW

A dusty moon: an owl sits in his tree.
Dawn: a din of birds rattles the tympanum
of his window. The self he would construct
becomes an owl in glass. Other selves
attend. Exiled from original places,
they choir the pears rotting on the ground.
Noon: a sprue of molten light spills
into the leaves. These are the words he speaks.
Their colors alter as they hover in the air.
After: the first edges of shadow, departures.
It is the wind that drums these changes: dolor.
Now: he is only his face in the window, copying
the wit of roots that nourish and decline.

WATCHING FOR TRUTH IN GALVESTON

The end of I 45 is the end of your life.
That homeless psycho, with his cart and beard,
shouts history you should count: in 1900
the dead rose from their boggy graves and floated
in their coffins, Beloved Sticks and Flotsam.
Where heaven oozes down to homeless crazies
granite slabs impound a dreadful tide,
but not the twisted wind. You're in the eye.
It's God's truth that circles in the steamy sky.

AFTER THE HURRICANE

the horizon breaks its seam
wide as his island.
Gulls ski down wind
over a pewter tide.
Wind-riven branches
fret the lawns.
Pink hibiscus open their virgin lips
to the beaks of chirming birds.
His feet in wreckage and mud,
head in the sky,
He breathes as deep as his birth.
It's day one.

CREPUSCULUM

The sky lies level on the Gulf of Mexico,
its spent light prismed by a wheel of dust
into fractions of vermillion. Obsessed joggers
rack their limits. Homing pick-up trucks
recite, *solfeggio*, their fumy run.
The last swimmers climb the granite rocks.
He waits the planet's turn, salutes the sun
and crosses the wall toward a furrowed dark.
"Not yet," he says, and waits for one more dusk.
"The sky is a lonely calendar. It's time,
my love, to muse under its luminous husk.
Anon, the moon will melt our motionless limbs."

DRIVING NORTH

for Paul Engle

He drove north again to the end of your life.
The tall maples were out, hills green once more,
the city newer and the same. The shacks
along the river were levelled long ago,
and those who made first soundings there are strewn
along the banks and towns of other codes.
Your Chinese consort bowed to your silent profile
and bade you on the Way. Farewell, old friend.
He owes you much. Vandals wreck us all.
Where names scatter like bowled-over pins in an alley—
Shelley, Thomas, Martin, Lowell, McGuire—
angels in crumpled grass announce this truth:
time sacks the past to a final disorder.
Dinosaurs climb from the Gulf, their ancient flora
turned black on the sand and on the granite wall.
Wind and salt corrode the chiselled intervals.

HISTORY ACCORDING TO AN ORDINARY MAN

for Ellen More

After the caves and crags and ziggurats,
we gave our voices to sticks and talking crows.
In moveable forests of lances and banderoles,
the armies marched till fields were caulked with gore.
Alexander, Darius, Alaric, Ivan, Pizarro—
what auguries fell, unhinged from galaxies?
Now the reverends whisper into the snail of the ear
and self-anointed oracles rant on screen.
And still the scheming chiefs attend their noise,
the innocent forfeit reason and their lives.

INTERIOR SEASONS

Ecco summer's sum along the bayou:
humid day expires in humid night.

An ordinary man, hostage to duplicitous
heaven, waits inside his hutch, himself,

for candid summer, the idea of summer, hops
in deliberate ripening, gradients to wisdom.

Autumn, when it comes, will take the sated
summer's place in strictest calibrations

of lessening light, imperiled cranes in flight,
leaves in scarlet champlevé, pifferos

and rising drafts from the squally water.
A northern man, estranged by tropical suns,

devises a northern mind that opens to autumn,
and winter's consummations. His sense of self

becomes a climate's sense, its very interior:
a diamond's culet in the purest sky.

He is not at odds with sudden turnings and mizzles
as summer gives way, the spilling poplars' gamboge,

a cricket's familiar brisance under his casement,
a bird's cadence at the burst and fall of a day,

the perse skies gathering. It is his proper
season then, his northward anima.

HE WAKES TO BELLS AND ROCKETS

"Once, in a borrowed chalet,
we clinked champagne and sang
to a williwaw of hail
against the stuttering shutters.
We skied down a dazzle of light.
We let the fire fall low
and loved, blind to seasons.
Now, at the end of clamor,
we rise from the numbed hours
to a morning streaked like a comet.
Mountains have slipped from our eyes.
Our years are tracked by flares
that crackle and shoot in the brain
as they slope to their separate darks."

A WHITE HORSE

When he sees a white horse in a Mexican field,
he remembers the pale horses felled by lightning,
their legs rigid in the electric air,
their sheltering tree split into its roots.
Beyond the grazing horse, he sees a cluster
of whitewashed tombs falling to native dust.
The sky is empty. There is no being in sight.
Wind bows the grass in the field and lifts
the white horse above the midget houses
of the dead. It drifts to the end of Mexico.
These images haunt like ancient photographs.

OBSTINATE GEEZER

Wake up, old guy! Let Easter spin to the sun!
Clomp your clumsy polka one more time!
Earth is blowing, *da capo*, its ancient horn!

FOXED

Foxed like an old book, his face pends
from the bare ball of his head as though to lose
its final seam. He runs free in the noose
of his past, so far, and back, and free again.
He rewrites history, but it comes to bad ends.
The faces in his face wear him to booze.
That fragrant woman whose hair brushed his nose
swims in his eye immutable until he's spent.

Angels of his fancy hover and leer.
He clings to sleep to make his fables true.
The edges of the real crack his sight.
The crone of now cackles in his ear.`
The inexorable morning befuddles him with light.
Concoctions are not enough. The day is mute.

THE HOUSE

His house, and not his house.

He looks out the second story window over a delinquent
    garden,
rooftops downhill to the sea.

She sits in her wicker chair.
A book has escaped her lap.

Her right hand curls,
the right side of her face is drawn down.

"They've brought us to allegiance by deceit,"
Ratushinskya says.

It is everywhere the same.
The bougainvillaea pours down wildly from the porch.

It is the last time.

ON THE RIVER

As he rides the river his friends fall away.
What he sees in the water is what he always knew,

turned away and awry like lovers gone.
He is what he remembers, not what he sees

in the water. Water is this falling away
under his face, the truth of things unheld.

When he lifts his face he is no longer there.
He is only here, dreaming, riding the river.

AH!

Maples scull the wind.
Birds bruit their customary departures
from the shaded eaves.
A distant diesel blats its way
up the westward hill.
Light flickers through leaves,
and slats of jalousies
onto the wooden floor where he stands,
naked, aware of his breathing.
A downed sun slants up again
into a summer morning.

AN ARTIST IN WINTER

Oregon

This is the time he circles on the rim
of everything, with booze, demented love.
He sketches the length of his bones, seams of skin
under light that casts no shadow. Above
the salmon runs, rigs as long as trees
bring the mountains down to pulp and ply.
A current cold along deserted beaches
pushes the oilers north to where the sky
sits on the water. Snow-lidded mountain cones
wait in the clouds for the cracked earth to break
its crust and bend its bitter ash around
a planet. When the run-off descends its quarrelsome way
down gullies and mains, he daubs his sunken dreams:
a sunshot body, a sky above the trees.

IN THE JESUS STORE

Oaxaca, 1993

Nine times over Jesus dies, hanging
from sticks roped to the ceiling. For 1000 pesos
you can take him down and home and hang
him on your wall above the stereo.
Bloody holes for nails, a slit in the chest
for a spear, and wounded knees add living color
to the celebrated event. His loins are swathed,
of course. G rating, except for the violence
that happened long ago and far away.
Across the street, at the *carnecería*, other
carcasses hang on hooks. You can take home a gutted
lamb for dinner. Jesus will bless your meat,
your bread and wine, and provide for home security.

VIEW FROM THE TOP

From this high, boggy place a slow
trickle of water from newly melted snow
knits its way through grass, a keen pine scent
in thin air, to begin its long descent,
a shifty continent to a mineral sea.

Against this ancient circularity
he catches his breath, catching the past,
the dwindling turns of earth he has left,
the tall clock of the sun on his burnished head,
the living chain, the fecund, scattered dead.

DESERT PLACES

The road clutches the wall of the Sierra.
He descends into moonscapes:
cold lava, gravel, boulders,
the sun eclipsed behind him.

Desert is sky. It does not fall in blocks
between buildings
or leak through the branches of trees.
It rises everywhere

and the long valleys suffuse
with reds, purples, grays,
as the mountains climb into light or deepen in shadow,
the day sun-white between.

Through distances he listens to the successions of his being.
Is not his blood the sap
of this scrubby, wind-twisted bristlecone?
Here he thinks of dying.

His consciousness is a paw, a brightly colored feather,
a bone in gravel . . .
In this naked place
he couples with beginnings. Endings.

HE SPEAKS TO THE CRIADA AT THE PIED WALL

Mexico, 1993

Below the rood a serpent sucks your dust.
In niches holy sprays wait for just
ablutions. In or out, the wall is history
more than you can bear. There is no mystery
in the rites you do by rote. Instruments
are all there are. They make the desolate sense
of every day. The One who died for you
is dead. There's no one left to tell the truth.
They've all gone home to wait for something more.
At matins who'll come back to start your chores?
The saints are hardened to your shriveled pleas.
Everything's exactly as it seems.

WHAT HE SAW IN THE SCHOOL YARD

The children lay, dishevelled, fallen in a doze
in the midst of play. They, too, were made to do,
or not to do. Causes have their causes.
Minds were made to mind insistent noises.
One who listened emptied a clip at random
into a field of children loudly babbling.

A million years: the impetus to act
became a god. Words became the knack
of sayers. In one the claim stayed deep in mist.
In the pitch of his mind there was no hold of history
to keep him with another. He heard alone,
and fell into a past beyond his books.
The voice that bade him fire broke the way
to selves: murderer and the listening prey.

JACK OF ALL TRADES

Gravity's maestro, he trails its doleful gyres
to troll extravagant green, belted blue,
the warp of rain, snow to the steepest soffits.

A tracker as the day rusts to dark,
he circles in the sky's fatal reflections.

Strung to compose again a planet's din,
he attends the waves' incessant *ostinato*,
churchly Bach, that hardy thrush in his tree.

A ravelled past's rock-worn plunderer,
he counts its strata to his brackish genius.

The seed falls to an ordinary man,
en passant.
He waits for the last wind,
the last rosette of light.

Aorta, stoppled,
turned his father black.
White as bread,
his mother fluttered
a quizzical good bye.

A surprising tide
spates the grit of his mind
with salt
and bears back to its origin
a looking glass
of ebbing and ending.

Under bent starlight,
on a moving plate,
he stands at the break
of gravity and brine.

TO THE FLYER

for Howard Nemerov

Had you fallen then, muzzle down through strati,
caught in a moment's flare of the sloping sun,
toward a roiled Channel or Britain's bearded fields,
would you have been the poet you became—
lucid, insouciant, ironic, inventive, true—
maneuvering deftly through that fatal sky,
wit against gravity? Now, at last, the planet
claims you, but where you flew with few we read
the luminous blips of a singular *prince des nueés*.

1934 RECHERCHÉ

Montage before he sleeps: you are there,
upper left, overlapping someone

else, as usual. What did he expect?
Once you had a corner on his life.

He waited in the orchard all night long
and ran home through a potter's field at dawn.

When birds broke into lilts above the dead,
he cracked his pain against a mile of stones.

Now you are gone and his losses more
than he can tell. He waits again in the dark

until your image mingles with the rest,
and runs with birds that cry in alien trees.

LETTER TO NOBODY

The ordinary man has come from muck to mort.
He dials his number and gets a busy sound.
Yip yip over the fence, his dreams are noise.
Bibles, scruffy prophets, zinc clouds that never
went away, he carried that sky forever
on his thumb. Clumpy space has no beginning
and no end. His time is all his own.
In Dallas they're making a movie of a movie.
Here there's nothing to report: drugs,
malpractice, low scores, contaminated oysters.
He reads. He writes. His car, *c'est lui.*
Good bye. His ashes go to the bayou soon.

PRAISE FROM AN ORDINARY MAN

Relics remain, of course: the lonely relief
of a spire, occasional bells, quavering hopes
ascending in a closed vault, quaint beliefs
seen through glass stained to city soot.
Our fathers fathered this and split their minds
to hold their fearful images against all learning.
We are heirs of their ages, but not of their kind.
We walk what is left of their metaphysical burnings:
scathed cities, stripped wilds, wars without end.
Pray now for eagles and salmon, horizons of trees.
Our lives are rivers, Manrique said, that find
their death in the sea. Our lives are a clock of seasons.
We walk a planet's procession where nature has meaning
by praise. Praise owls and oaks and autumns and seas.

AN ORDINARY DOOR

An archway, and, beyond, a flight to a door,
a toy boat sailing the cracked tile of the floor—
an illusion of light beneath a crumbled sky . . .
The haunting image fastens in the eye:

a forsaken child that voyaged a world from here.
And now, at the limit of seas, the door is there
again, opening into a darkened room
where a black-clad mother sways to ancient runes.

Her dolorous clasp defines the end of journeys:
cleaving, bitter flight, foreboding return.
The ritual is complete: the child that drowned
comes home on the tide. The image scans full round.

ON ISLAMORADA

The day is not aware of motives, or grapes
as green as the sea off the sands of Islamorada,
or of the miniature roundness of the grapes,
or the erotic roundness of the mounting waves:
a still life in the eye of skin transparent
as glass in a bowl opaque as henna earth.
The picnickers are looking at the painter.
The women, unclothed, recline at ease. The men,
bearded, clothed, have other things to do.
The day has no intention. It floats away
as the bent earth turns. In languishing light, the grapes
become an enigmatic beryl. The bearded
men depart. The painter stays to limn
the nymphs turning phosphorescent in the sea.

SOMETHING ELSE

When the final earth fastens over him,
his friends, still loose, will remember one thing
or another: his quickness, say, to wit. Or madness.
Winter will fail, first crocuses lift from their graves
like bones to flare among the smoldered leaves.
The words in his mouth will savor of grubs and clay,
books go tawny and dumb. Seeds, of course,
will thrive in other places, repeating their kind.
What was real but once becomes untrue.
You can claim this is a life, but when
you tell it, it warps to something else, archaic
and droll, a cartouche, say, or a shriven stone.
No matter then: he will have forgotten his craft.

THE WIND FROM CANCUN

While he sits in his patio reading
worms are eating the pears that fell this morning
in the wind that blew from Cancun.
His attention separates from his book.
He watches the pears.
Stems crack and the earth pulls through the thick air.
There are too many pears for the worms.
The pears fall all day, even though the wind has stopped.

Somewhere, as far as Cancun,
a girl with dark hair is playing her guitar
and singing softly.
Her song is the one he has been waiting for.

IN THE PARK

There is some beauty in bizarre arrangements:
an old dame covered with pigeons that peck her bread
and drop their chalky guano on benches and grass,
their wings aflap in the breeze like dirty sails.
Here the homeless, at home as pampered pigeons,
convert their scavenged cans to bargain booze.
Walks and lamp poles measure the prostrate green
where children scream and strew their candy wrappers,
joggers jog their fat, dogs pee on trees,
lovers loiter, and the dealers pander.
Thus nature and the human are composed
in scenic dispositions of frightful concinnity.

A NATURAL HISTORY OF THE ORDINARY MAN

Where the mind is gritty beauty ensheathes.
What he made made itself, its gifts
accreting. There is no mete for these in his dreams.
With the first turning, a naked foot lifted,
contrapposto, stone grew deft and light.
The changes came with luminescence, jolts
of apprehension, gatherings of signs
in a gravelly mouth. Where he rode the shock
of storms white hibiscus kissed the waves.
The gods receded into the dark of meaning.
Hic jacet in the oyster bed the ashes
of one loosened from his swart beginnings.
As they settle at last against the silted tide,
his dense words glisten on their lunar shingle.

AN ORDINARY MAN'S ADVICE TO THE BIKER

for Kevin

The edges are always open. Wheels or wings
will lift you from the street like Evel Knievel.
The sky slides under your pedals. You ride the wind,
a kite without a string. Spumy seas
tilt and fall. The last gull dips and bends
the air back to the sweet smell of the shore.
The moment has no measure to the end.
The sun will tell you what you need to know.

WINTER

It is a thing in nature: black branches,
black water against snow. It is a time
before sound. It is composed in his eye.
He is the imperfection in this scene.
His nature is an antic miscellany
by Miró. The branches are a bicycle
unraveling. The snow is rolled into a moon.
An orange sun interferes with his face. His eyes
fly into a landscape of cartoons.
What is perfection? It is imperfection.
The thing in nature is death's photograph.

EN ROUTE TO YOU

Where seeds have blown to the luck of stony ground
a surf of flowers rolls against the road.
En route to you, he thinks of random junctions,
choices made as though the causes were known,
miracles that track an equinox,
sudden rains that gulch and bloom a desert.
"In fields," he says, "we're two in a million hawk weeds
whose colors dazzle and wither in the dirt.
The taken road that crossed a chance of flowers
marks our meantime as the time that matters."

RECOLLECTING YOU

He reconstructs you from dusty motes.
He reads you like the back of his soul.
Your image clots like rancid wine.
You loom and fade, a doppler effect,
or pend from every tumid storm.
When he says your lumpy name
a screw of fire turns in his throat.
He forgets you not, old dame.

SLEEP

He curls against the north. Flindery bones
thrum their slow complaints, a mortal self.
Boccherini spins down. He is harrowed
by landscapes of remembered snow. The moon
imprisons him in his window. He sinks to particulars,
this pain, that felicity. His crambos go
like a panic of not arriving. He cons the enigma
of his future. You say this. He says that.
His eyes congeal. His skull plays five guitars.
Diminished gods welcome him to absence.

LA VIEJA SPEAKS TO THE ORDINARY MAN

Oaxaca

I look and cannot see.
Stories told in the smoky dark
are cold as ashes.
When the sky was high as an eagle
we made the signs on wheels.
Under mounds, in looted tombs,
in empty trees where hawks have feasted,
our ghosts have gone away.
The past cuts arroyos in my face.
The wind makes dust a seal against my breath.

LETTER TO HUGO FROM THE ORDINARY MAN

Along the Gulf, 1988

Air is swamp. Where ground is high enough,
it's a bait shop or a bar, shacks on stilts
like spindly birds. Rusty shrimpers wobble
on a dirty tide. Rheumatic oaks cling
like washed-out whores to their familiar streets.
Isn't this the same forgotten scene you squinted
once on roads that disappear toward Butte?
Welcome to no home. We lean through one
sad town and another. Their cancelled names bleach
into the whiteness of your eye. The last graffito
flakes to dust before you say good bye.

THE ORDINARY MAN SAYS FORGET IT

That tune you carry like a plague, played
by Bechet, '40s, back in Boston, breaks
out when the early hours are long and rotten.
Your fractured body wails. Years forgotten
glide by like surrendered lovers dancing slowly.

Sober up, baby, it's only a case of lows,
a bass fiddle twanging in the smoke.
That beat is someone's finger on your pulse.
Boston's gone, and all the lying blues.
Now is then when Bechet stops on cue.

RAINBOW

> He loops a yellow line
> through the air,
> dropping the fly
> precisely
> at the beginning
> of a riffle
> where
> a mythical trout
> lies waiting,
> a flash of sun
> shimmering
> through the water,
> flaunting
> in its momentary prism
> images of everything.

FALL

> A morning of birds
> cries up the turning trees;
> sea mammals gambol
> on satiny rocks;
> a fragrance of apples
> surfeits the orchards;
> the composer's L'Autunno,
> the poet's Valediction,
> requite a season's memory.
> We linger at the temple at Sounion
> in the final cleft of a luminous sea
> to praise the beauty and sadness of things
> in the conceiving eye,
> the surprise of *appoggiaturas*
> in the mind.

TO ROBERT ORTH, BURMA, 1944

You fell out of a plane. Later we heard about you
in Calcutta. Pushing supplies through
the door of a DC3, you got slammed
by the wind. The bundles floated down, ammo,
food, our monthly ration of bad scotch.
Did you fall with the blossoming chutes, clutching
for their gentled descent? Nobody saw you go.
The jungle hides its fauna fast below
its billion leaves to blend with sodden ground.
No lines over land, we had to count
on your drops to carry us all our maniacal way
to the River Irrawaddy and Mandalay.
We found the booze and drank it, all unknowing
long ago. Those of us here and there
still drink to everything in earth and air,
and you, between, who kept us bloody going.

CECI N'EST PAS UN POEME

The painter is practicing his dismembering art.
The ordinary man hasn't combed his hair in a month.
The women are spending the day at the movies. The men
are drinking cappuccino and champagne.
They talk of pasta, poetry, and children.

A bright-eyed tree is watching from the street.
Illuminated billboards sever the sky.
A rock in the room is key to painted mountains,
where the poet is teaching a snowy owl to hoot.
An unexpected answer is waiting at the door.

STONE CREEK

Green boiling white over slick stone,
going green again like sleep, moving deep,
clouds drifting across the green, gravity gone,
his face looking down looking up at him,
his mother's face in an old photo, round,
stray hairs over her eyes, beside his dark,
Homburg-hatted father, by a gravestone,
caught there, maybe twenty, before his birth . . .
The sky riffles her face and they are gray.
Weight of water, weight of a child, the earth
silting down to the begetting sea again . . .
Here, where nature works her ancient circle,
he faces the coming down, the green going deep,
in motion over stone, into sleep.

AFTERWORD

Listeners will hear themselves . . .

Poetic intentions and circumstances are simply autobiography. In the event that the reader is interested in the intentional and technical particulars of this poet's life, I will say that when I write I make what Robert Lowell used to call "jumps" in order to sustain the discoveries essential to the poem's evolution. Using images, juxtapositions, irony, sinewy language, *et alii*, I work through many revisions to refine the poem to a formal disposition. Nothing singular here, save that, through the *persona* of the book, the voice and the occasions of the poems are mine. Though I was engrossed in making the poems ("getting them right") and not in a prospective audience, I now, as I must, offer them to readers other than myself. Poems, of course, unveil their own intentions; and the reader's attending to them will, properly, establish their meaning and open them to judgements according to the reader's own touchstones and expectations.

I began writing in the fourth grade with love poems to my teacher. She was as encouraging as she could be. Following those early days, of course, emotions have gotten more complex and enduring (losing, inevitably, both their purity and their transciency), and the poems have gotten tougher and more wary, as, indeed, has the poet, now in his seventy-eighth year, retired to a semi-tropical island, and still writing.

CHRISTOPHER BURSK

The One True Religion

CHRISTOPHER BURSK, the boy holding the branch in the photograph, teaches at Bucks County Community College and is a volunteer counselor in the Bucks County Corrections System. The recipient of Guggenheim, NEA, and Pew Fellowships, he has previously published four books of poetry.

CONTENTS

SECTION ONE

I

One talking, one listening,
one asking questions so the other would not stop.
Did she appear in a vision to the older boy
or to the younger? *Fighting Pehbee,*
a goddess
as distracted and angry as weather.
This was how they played
on their way home from school,
making supper by themselves,
keeping the same story going for weeks,
to turn rain on the roof
into arrows, shadows
into dogs sleeping at their feet,
each terror of their day—ordinary beatings,
doors slammed, a house in ruins—changed
at night into glorious acts, a fortress
under siege.
Their mother had been pressed to the ground,
held there
by a man they'd never seen before,
a man who had brushed them aside
like branches in the way.
He had a needle, a black bag.
Their father had watched
as if someone was holding his arms.
Do something! they begged their mother.
Make the man stop!

II

Thus the last daughter of Brem escaped
north, past the tribes covered by fur,
people whose breath melts ice,
And when finally she was too chilled and weary

to journey further,
she lay down in a field
and slept for three days and woke at night
and saw before her a statue
so real
at first she mistook it for the goddess herself.
She could hear the winds cry from the stone mouth.
And when it was morning
she looked down
and though she had not realized she was with child,
she saw now that she had given birth
to two sons,
he who would become Jeren Rothar,
he who would be Rowal, keeper of the sacred spring.
And the first word on their lips
was the name of the goddess.

III
Even now the two boys crawl up into the attic,
sky so black through the narrow window
it's easy to forget they are in a house
on a street, in a town,
and the darkness draws them
towards it as they chant
Pehbee, Pehbee,
not so she can hear and come back,
but for the sound's water
rubbing on stones,
sharp, jagged rocks
dangerously smoothed.

Who are you? my mother asked
when I was five.
What could I say? *I am your son.*

I'd become as puzzling to my mother
as unexpected rain.

My brother was a rank odor,
a stain that would not be washed out.
Up to no good.
Bad. Troubled. Disturbed. A disturbance.
Written up,
reported, famous in third grade, infamous in seventh.

I was jealous,
felt betrayed.
But what had he done but succeed
at what he was good at?
What had my mother ever done except to forget?

She cried by the window.
She cried by the door.
I found her on curbs and led her home.

Everyone in town knew.

Some day I'll show them,
I'd tell the air when I was nine. When I was fifteen
I was still talking to the trees.

I'd work three times harder than I had to,
four times. Skinny,
I kept eating.
Scared, I tackled the cruelest boy.

If it started storming, I stayed outside
weeding the garden,
raking up the leaves.

Who are you? the wind would ask
and the rain wanted to know.

ONE MATCH

One match
all each of us was allowed.
I was to pile my favorite toys in the fireplace,
everything I loved that burned,
my paper crown and sword,
my stuffed animals.
If my brother had to sacrifice,
so did I.
He wouldn't let me go till we had watched
everything sink to ash.
We looked into the flames till there was nothing
to hold our gaze,
nothing but the wind
moving through the embers
like an army of beggars,
breezes bickering over the spoils.
Night pulled at us from all sides.
We had one match remaining between us.
Mine. My brother took it,
kept it
for when we could not bear the dark,
when we had almost completely forgotten
what light was.

It is 1949. There is no one hungry
in our town, but still
we go from door to door.
My mother presses against the screen
and if the lady of the house refuses to let her in,
denies her anything—
a signature, money—
my mother offers up scarred breasts,
necks horrifyingly thin; naked, bloated children.
We don't leave
till the woman takes a leaflet; every house gives up
far more than it had intended.
Waiting, I don't dare hum or whistle,
but stare straight into the shadowy hall,
deep into a house where a cat is crying.
I'm five. We're fighting on the side of Armenian rebels,
Algerians, the hibakusha,
begging food for starving Germans.
I think my mother the noblest person
and I'm her *money bags*
she tells me. I fold dollars into my belt pouch.
My shorts sag with pennies, nickels, dimes.
The weight of the coins presses against my legs.
We do not turn the lights on at home
in any room but one.
We keep the house dark
as if there is some deep interior to it
at whose borders we must move carefully
so as not to startle those ghostly children
in my mother's pamphlets,
old refugee women with their sad, long dresses,
toothless, shaved men
too frail to harm anyone now.
In the kitchen we turn our pockets inside out.
Here is where I learn to count,

with my fingers,
the little meowing scrape
of quarters across the kitchen table,
a splurge of nickels,
pennies crowded together like just liberated prisoners
        of war,
dimes thin and imperious,
old dollars soft in my palms,
a fortune in rushed signatures, curled-up petitions,
the accumulated riches
we've put off reckoning all day
for the evening's pleasure,
my mother's and mine, of sorting and counting,
stacking and folding, counting again,
a fabulous wealth ours,
all ours
to give away.

THINKING CHAIR

Don't move. Don't even think
of moving. His mother
has dragged him by the ear to a chair. He sits
on his hands, feels the soft weight
of his whole body pressing down.
Do you think I'm stupid?
Do you imagine I won't know
if you move even one inch from this chair?
His mother pulls the door shut as she speaks
so the click of the lock
is her last word. She's gone.
She'll be gone all day.
The boy could get up, he could

open the window,
drop to the ground. Walk away.
He rocks back and forth
on his hands. His body
is light
on his right hand, heavy
on his left. Then it's the left
freed; the right pressed down
flat to the bone. Each bone
aches and protests
till the right's allowed
up, to breathe
and question the little blessed latitude
it's been granted.

YOU ARE GOING TO DIE

Really! You are going to die.
I'm not making this up.
Why do you think daddy got you that bicycle
when it's not even your birthday?
You cut a few strands of my hair each day
and examine them under your microscope,
study my urine for signs of blood,
keep records, noting weight loss,
the color of my nails.
After my bath I must stand before you.
Look how shriveled your scrotum is,
how dry and cracked your elbows get.
What more proof do you need?
When I'm gone, you promise
you'll publish a book. I'll be famous.
Readers will weep over the boy

who never let his father know
he knew he was dying.
We pull down the blinds
and in the dark I choose what to wear in the coffin,
which of my favorite toys
you are to sneak under its lid. You practice
what you'll say at my funeral.
At school I give away my sandwich, my cookies.
Even you begin coaxing me, *Eat! Eat!*
bringing me saltines you've buttered
just as I like them, cocoa so hot
it has the little skin I love to scrape off the top.
Why does your brother never leave his room?
Father draws you aside. What
do you say to him? That you bragged
to your friends that you could talk
your kid brother into believing anything? After nights of
letting me crawl into your bed
and weep against your side,
how can you turn to me, one morning,
as you know you must,
and tell me all those tears preserved in tissues and dated,
the long lists of what I've willed away,
our days of preparation,
were wasted, my hope
for immortality unfounded,
my life not nearly as precious as I'd thought?

Would you brush my hair?
my mother would say
but what she really meant was
Would you listen to my sorrows?
Would you put away your toys
long enough for me
to tell you how I hurt?

I'd go to work, as business-like
as the bristles, tug
at each snag, pull the brush through till nothing
stopped it, till it fell
as light does through a woman's hair,
till it seemed I, not the light, made it shine.

It's so cold. Don't go back outside.
Stay in here by the fire,
my mother would beg. *Sit.*
Let me put the water on.
A cup of hot cocoa would do us both good,
meaning *Let me tell you what I dreamed last night.*

The queen lifted a goblet to her lips,
then held it out,
tipping it so the sun turned even its dark
poison into a bright disc.
How could such a simple gesture possibly hurt?
She was offering a gift
no one else could give.

What are you playing?
my mother would ask, meaning
Open the door. Meaning
Hate what I hate
or *Take my hand, walk with me to the edge of the world.*

He wakes to what sounds like the wind
and finds his mother
throwing herself against doors
as if she doesn't know how else to open them,
as if she's forgotten how to turn a knob.
She pushes the boy's father aside.
The wind is married to no one.
Can his Dad afford to stay home all day
to make sure
she doesn't put her hand through the window?
No, the boy holds his mother
to a schedule, wakes her, reads to her,
brings her lunch on a tray,
leads her away from open windows,
a drawer full of knives. On some nights
his father does not come home,
and the whole world grows so dark and vast
he can't imagine anyone living in it
and then he hears his mother singing
to herself. Words
that don't make sense,
wind trapped in a cave, a song
he carries into sleep.
One day he wakes to his mother screaming,
bearing her bleeding arm from room to room
and the next day the window is fixed.
His mother has vanished.
Living with her
had been like trying to coax the rain into falling
more softly, to persuade the wind
to stay in one place. Now what is there
to fill his days? He reads everything he can find
on hurricanes, ships
swept against rocks, families marooned,
cyclones setting them down

in enchanted lands. It's his turn
to be the one lost
and to look out at an ocean too immense
for anyone to cross, though he tries,
and the breakers thrust him back.
No hope of rescue? Okay,
then he's free
to make his own breakfast, his own stories,
the one pined for,
the castaway,
combing the beach for what the waves bring in.

A WAY TO PASS THE TIME

The strangulations and poisonings
began as a way of filling the empty moments
in the doctor's waiting room
or in the backseat on the way home.
We'd hijack a plane or kidnap a baby
and one more afternoon would pass in rescue
and revenge. Especially good at germ warfare
we spread contagion differently
each time, so it'd be harder
to find a cure. What was a day
without danger, a little calculated
cruelty to overcome? Let's play, we'd say,
and it would take all morning to get out the maps,
draw up the treaties
we'd eventually break, mark off new boundaries,
swap secret powers. It was hard work
being both hero
and bad guy, a civil service
of villains and victims. A simple assassination plot
demanded passports, a portfolio

of documents. We surveyed the land, studied blueprints,
the exact measurements
for where to plant a bomb. Blocked off exits.
No one appreciates how much effort is required
to blow up a skyscraper
or burn a village
or enslave a population. Soon it was not enough
to invade a country. We had to
build roads there, establish a postal service,
set up a banking system,
teach the people to love the very army
that had seized their homes.
Even before we'd conquered one planet
we were already building rockets
to subdue another. Go to school?
We didn't have the time. We rarely left the house.
Whom could we trust
in our absence
to see the poor were fed, the rivers dammed,
justice was done?
We had obligations now, an empire
to maintain, a bureaucracy
to see to, a world
that could not do without us.

USURPER

A title with a long lineage.
Say the name
and a boy feels its mantle fall over his shoulders.
He is Richard the Hunchback,
Alfred the Twisted,
Bloody Prince John. Judas. All of time opens up
and he steps through
into history
as if now it belongs to him, only him

and his martyred brother.
O the terrible injustice of it.
Dragged out of bed.
Locked in a tower.
Sentenced to hang for a crime
you did not commit.
Led to the gallows, swearing your innocence.
Your own brother placing your neck
in the noose.

O falsely accused.
O cruelly betrayed.
No pleasure greater.

MATTHEW 3:13-17

Not Jesus on the cross,
but Jesus the boy
by himself, shivering, gazing into the water,
his hand cupping his scrotum,
the puzzling extra organ
attached outside his body.
I could believe in this Jesus.
Just saying the name gives me pleasure,
a word as soft
and adjustable as genitals in the palm,
a breath let out slowly.
I like to imagine Jesus
standing by the river
as if he'd never seen so much water moving headlong
in one direction.
All his weight is on his back foot.
Any moment he'll lift his arms,
step out onto the water.

MOUTHRA

Mouthra, Mouthra, the boys intoned,
the younger one's word
for the water that threw itself again and again
at the same hard place
till what once had been stone
was air, a gate flung open, centuries ago
though the brook was still galloping out of its dark stall,
still shaking its mane.
Here was light's sister, water
reminding even the largest rocks
what it was like to run loose.

Here the boys built a temple on both banks,
set stones in the brook
so they could step into the midst of pure motion.
In early December, in late February,
they smashed holes in the ice
and plunged their arms down into the brook,
held their hands there,
fingers splayed out,
till the cold became part of them, its ache
a test of loyalty, a kind of prayer,
till they believed
the water was rushing through their whole bodies.
But, O the Kings of Thavigea were wily,
the older brother explained.
Right after they conquered Brem
they realized they had to subdue its gods as well
and so they laid the first stones of their city
over the sacred spring,
locked the brook up
in pipes, the only water now
buried in darkness,
water at everyone's beck and call,
even the slaves' servant. The Thavigean rulers knew
what waits on a person
soon stops
being sacred. In the woods
the boys took the largest stones they could find
and brought them down on the pipes.
Iron had to give.

The men are dressed in dark uniforms.
Marching through town, they make the sound
scythes do
as the tall grass falls away
in great swaths. He can no more move out of their path
than the grass can. Women
and children are being herded
into pens. He is in his pajamas
and his pants have snagged
on the fence he is trying to climb.
His father is standing on a hill
like a man who has just put something into motion
and then lost interest.
He sees him so clearly
he can make out the insignia on his father's buttons.
Below his father, arms rise and fall, exactly together
as if a metronome were moving them.
There are too many bodies,
too many women wailing for anyone to pick out a boy's
shrill voice, *Father!*
Father! The word for all a boy's anguish.
Waking, he follows his cry to the surface
as if underwater, thrashing,
fighting loose.
He grips the edge of the bedsheet, bites down
to stop the shriek
before it actually leaves his mouth,
reaches and wakes his father.
He holds the cry
in his head; it pushes
against the back of his skull.

For an entire week, scared
our mother would never be released from the hospital
my brother and I watched
with our father from the window he loved best,
the one that opened like a door.
After supper
he put aside his Greek dictionaries, his translations,
and made us look up at the stars
till we believed we had the power to reach them.
Those nights our homework went unchecked
he seemed lordly
as he swung first my brother onto the back of Pegasus,
and then me,
and then he pulled himself up behind
and wrapped his arms around us.
We are crossing the burning floors of suns,
he said. *We are walking on beds of starlight.*
Don't be afraid, Christopher,
Jack. We are riding bareback now
on a horse with wings.

THE WOMAN LIGHT LOVED

Once there was a woman who lived in a castle.
She'd wake
and discover the light sleeping at her feet
like an old, tamed lion.
She'd open the shutters and there it'd be
perched on the sill, so forlorn
she'd have to let it in.
No matter how deep she retreated into the castle
it found a way to her.
The light refused to fall on anyone
but her. Now here's the rub, my children.
Perhaps she should have suspected
once the robes of majesty
fell over her husband's shoulders,
once the crown had settled on his head,
he'd betray her. It wasn't his fault.
Perhaps each time he touched her
he felt the light's touch
before him
already on her throat, on her breasts.
Hadn't she taught him to think
and speak like a king?
She had given him her body
—that is to say,
her courage—and borne him sons
not so different from you, my princes.
But a king could not humble himself
before anyone. And so
of course
he set her in a tower. He locked her there
with her sons.
Let the light buy them bread.
Let the light lace their shoes
and read stories to them.
Let the light pick on their bones.

I

By morning his mother had thrown away the brushes
and started painting
with her fingers. Alizarin,
scarlet, flashes of yellow
flames rushed out of her hands, off the canvas,
and onto the living room walls.
Streaks of crimson. Cadmium orange.
What was keeping his father?
His mother was painting the windows now.
There'd be no way he could clean up this mess
in time. Soon
the whole house would be covered in flames.
Stop it.
Dad will be home any minute. Please.
You've got to stop.
Living with his mother
was like living in a house where the sun had been forced
to take up residence.
How could anything that brilliant make do
in such small quarters?

II

Here she does not shriek
or reach for the sleeves of boys, his classmates.
He does not have to loosen her grip
on the train station gates. Instead
there is a long, intelligent silence
between them. Once again
his mother is pale and beautiful
as she always is in the hospital.
She has her own room
in this mansion whose grounds stretch to fields of aster,
a high wrought-iron fence,
and a small gated bridge
with a tunnel below, barred too.

Here only the stream slips free.
In the shade his mother and he crouch
and dip stones in the water,
find the dark weather buried in each.
He knows better
than to beg his mother to come home.
Why would she ever want to
leave her grand estate?

SECTION TWO

In the beginning there was light
and there was darkness
and the dark loved the light
as a glutton loves the feast set before him,
as a tidal wave relishes the village it is about to devour,
as the assassin admires the pale throat
it intends to slit. Out of the dark
were created men, shadows
like waves that refused to fall
back into the great watery mass we know as darkness now,
and because they were the first
they were free to name everything
that came afterwards:
their children, the weather, the changing of the light,
flowers and birds. They decided
what sounds to fasten
to what shapes, for example
which winged, pollen-sipping creature to call
vermin, which to imagine
lovely, what to hate,
what to hoard,
what to spit out, what to savor.
These first men were no different from any
who followed: they raised armies,
built walls around their cities
and over their towers and on their masts
hoisted flags.
Everything dark they hid.
They painted it the color of light
on water, light
on a field of wheat. The halls of the palace.
The stadium. The baths. The pawnshops.
Even the prisons.
But under everything they knew
lay darkness. Even their language,

each word created out of darkness.
Shadows, deceit, ruins. Perhaps
light was not meant to rule the earth,
to preside in courts. Evening
after evening, it gave up its throne,
wilted, let its empire be eaten away.

THE DARK AGES

How much am I expected to endure?
Our mother swept our father's cold supper off the table,
then hers, then ours,
then tipped the whole table over
and pushed us aside.
She shut the door
as if she intended never to open it again.
We cleaned up as fast as we could,
then went through the house, turning out the lights,
pulling the blinds.
In the dark between our beds
my brother had me repeat the names of kings,
the dates of battles. Each night
we made history,
adding a little more, a plague, an inquisition,
my brother telling it to me,
I saying it back to him. And if we still couldn't sleep
we lit a candle and took out the scrolls
we'd stolen from our father's desk,
his next book's proofs
perfect for proclamations.
On a single galley sheet we could fit the entire lineage
of a kingdom from its earliest
beginnings to the very moment
our pens stopped writing, all of recorded time

rolled up tight
and held in our hands,
the War of the Iris and the Dahlia,
the Blessed Infant's War.
My brother bent over his work,
elbow on the map he was drawing,
brow pressed hard on the palm of his free hand,
fingers gripping hair,
tugging hard at the scalp
as if trying to rip out the world from his brain,
Meregini, New Meregini,
the Vartesian Archipelago,
each island distinguishable
from the last: a broken shard of pottery,
a leaf gnawed to lace,
a torn bootsole, a bead of water,
the turbulent seas
hidden under our beds.
What is this craziness?
What are you doing with your father's papers?
I am going to teach you a lesson you'll never forget.
The Bronze Age,
the Iron Age, the Age of Exile,
ripped in half,
then these halves ripped again,
all our father's words,
all our history
in shreds. Then our mother rocking on the floor,
trying to fit the pieces back together.
Now see what you've made me do?
We led her back to bed.
We had work ahead of us.
Not till we had re-named each river
would it flow,
not till we had noted its precise altitude
would each mountain range rise again.
We didn't have much time.

Each glorious rescue,
each thwarted assassination plot—
to save the world
we had to recall it
down to its smallest detail, fireflies,
water-striders, crickets and brush-me-asides,
hearthfires and harvest songs.
We could feel the entire planet already growing dark.

ASHES

Jack danced in our room.
He was a flame leaping from bed to bed.
When our mother came in, there he was
naked and slippery
jumping out of her reach,
flouting her in all the windows.
No wonder she hit him,
knocked him to the floor,
threw herself against him
as if to snuff him out.
But you could no more persuade my brother
than you could teach a spark
loose in the house.
How can you blame fire
for doing what it was born to do?
I was ashes that had taken the shape of a boy.
I kept still. A false move,
a rash gesture
and I'd scatter, be nothing,
blow away.

ATALANTA

My father read to us
from the Greek. It was how the gods talked.
We thought it was our father's language too
and he was just being kind
when he spoke to us
in ours. Little armored insects,
phalanxes of letters
like tiny soldiers with miniature bows and arrows,
marched across the page.
Even my brother who could read
couldn't puzzle them out. *No!*
I'd shout, reaching out my hand
to pluck the apple, push
Atalanta forward, the swift-footed,
proud maiden
stooping to pick up not one, not two,
but three
polished apples dropped by a crafty suitor
with a silly name. *No!*
Certain stories I didn't want to end
the way they had
before, kept hoping to the very last word
they wouldn't. It was my father's fault.
He could have read it again, sent a rabbit
through the brush, distracted Aphrodite's hounds,
startled her,
diverted Acteon's eyes
from what he couldn't help gazing at,
the goddess wholly naked, reaching for her quiver.
My father could have demanded Daedalus
fly just above
his boy, his wings
casting cool shadows on Icarus,
the wax never melting.

Each leaf was covered with silver glintings
we thought at first were hairs,
a bristling fur. That should have been a clue
to the wisteria's dark
sinewy intentions. One morning we awoke
and found the world
choked, even our tree fort
over-run, vines
wound so many times around the trunks,
branch after
branch was brought low by a gorgeousness
so extensive it could not be pruned,
would not be cut back, a reckless appetite
that devoured clothesline,
swing set, television antennae.
No wind could stop it.
No rain beat it back, the wisteria
an armada of flowers
heading up every channel open to it, a fleet
full sail, armed,
horned, prehistoric, each petal
with its own battering ram
and a cargo of white
tough seeds
to be spread like the gospel
at any cost. An ancient hunger.
A savage rapture. The vines stretching
across the yard, rooting
into the ground, seizing
what rightfully belonged to the grass,
gripping hard
and refusing to let go
till all the earth was theirs.

Two boys are talking.
One has wrapped a quilt around himself.
It fans out at his feet like the folds of a great dress.
The other has fallen to his knees
on a rock so wide and flat
it looks like a perfect spot for a sacrifice.
In the stone there is a small, dark pool of rainwater.

These are tears.
My tears. Drink them, the older brother says.
Drink them all.

The stronger boy lets go of the weaker one's wrist.
Someone has to pay.
Someone has to die.
He picks up a knife,
rubs it against the rock as if sharpening it,
drags it lightly down the other boy's arm,
presses it to his abdomen.
He leans over his brother
like a doctor
explaining each step of a difficult operation.

He is so close to him
he could be whispering into his ear.
He could be tucking him into bed.

The point is for both to believe
the one might actually push the knife in,
the other might really feel a pain
so deep he could never recover.

Strung up by the ankles. Beaten.
Pressed under great slabs of stone.
Buried up to the neck
in sand, face smeared with honey
for the ants to feast on. Our tongues cut off.
Our eyes plucked out.
It was never enough. We grew bored
with being tied to rocks and left for the tides,
the tedium of surviving falls from thousand foot cliffs.
Fed up with comic book fiends
who could think of nothing better
than poisoning the city's water supply,
we wanted to be tested,
our every move anticipated,
every contest put in doubt.
We wanted a wickedness equal to the task,
men who looked like chunks of rock,
like jagged glass,
always a worse scoundrel hidden
behind the arras,
a ringleader, unrepentant,
unswerving,
no one more true to his principles
than a villain. Soon it was his voice
that started coming out of each of our mouths,
that odd sense of betrayal
an assassin feels when the one he's trying to kill
refuses to behave
and die. We ended up spending more time
wiring bombs
than defusing them. Who wants to be the duped
when he could be the duplicitous?
The kindly, inarticulate King
when he might be the Prime Minister,
silver-tongued,

scheming? The mastermind.
Murder! Pillage!
What a wonderful world this was!

THE HEIR APPARENT

No, I was not the one who held the cup
to your lips, urged you to drink,
saying, *Your lips must be parched.*
Your health, King!
But I watched
as the cup was polished with poison, rubbed so hard
it shone till a man could not help but want
to press his lips to gold
that gleaming. You held the dark liquid in your mouth
as if to offer us a last chance
to be decent,
to be fair. Then you swallowed
as if it would be bad manners not to.

Even then it was not too late.
I could have rushed to you.
What harm had you caused me?
You wore your beauty like a soft light
you could not shake off.
If you had not already been king
we'd have crowned you so.
Yes, even I
who begrudged you all your gifts
and the grace with which you bore them.

I did not hold the flowers' fragrance
against them. But they died
on their own. Every year.
They did not need to be poisoned.

Jeren it was, wise father of the Brem,
who in the midst of the great drought
when the eye of Far burned upon the city of Vaneb,
went to the Insang Tower
built a thousand years before
the Brem had first seen the red sails of the Thavigeans,
and Jeren climbed the three hundred stairs
saying prayers at each holy step
until he reached the highest.
There, Far spoke to Jeren: *The World is mine.*
Even so I began in the burning desert
in the fire of Lugmir,
in a place no creature can approach.
I must live in the distance. In the emptiness.
You must lead my people out of the land of Thavigea
and into the desert.
Beyond are the western mountains
and beyond the mountains
lies a land of wide rivers and sweet grapes.
No man had ever crossed the desert.
No man could live within the emptiness
which lay beyond the mountains.
What shall I say to the people?
asked Jeren
after his heart sank under his Lord's heavy commandment.
Then Far laughed.
Tell my people to put on their holiday clothes,
to drink wine instead of water
and dance in the dust.
Let their oppressors marvel that in the midst of drought
the Brem burned their houses,
sold their most beloved possessions,
gave up even their shoes
and on this, the Day of Deliverance,
walked into the desert.

You stop. Consider
never moving from the spot you've chosen
as being far enough
from where you left and safer
than where you are headed.
Sometimes you are a warrior.
Sometimes an outlaw
whose renegade gang would gladly die by his side.
Bring me the tyrant's head!
you'll say
to the trees. Sometimes you are an old man
telling his secrets to the few who bend over his deathbed,
those who must carry on his work.
Or you are a scientist
and the planet is about to collide with another planet
and you are the only one
with the power to change the earth's axis.
But sometimes you are just a child and cold
and too scared to go back
and too scared to go forward.
The rain's under your collar
again, keeps finding
the exact same spot on your neck
no matter how tight you pull your coat.
Count on this: the passage of time
solves nothing. The temperature
will keep dropping. The closer it gets to zero
the less use the night has
for anything human, anything that hopes
to make a stand.
The world stretches apart
till you wonder how anyone crosses even the smallest
distance, say between this stretch of shadows
and that spiked
clump of bushes, this burned out streetlight

and that dark, judgmental oak.
You've got to get moving
you say to yourself. *Now.*
Do you want to stay in one place
all your life? You do
and you don't.

THE FLOOD

We wait for the hired woman
to shut her door and then
her light and then the house itself
grows quiet as a ship that has turned off its engines.
Everywhere that isn't desk or bureau or chair
is ocean. A flood covered as far
as we can see. Capsized,
we clutch the sides of our beds.
Wave after wave strikes us, tries to
drag us away. *Don't*
let go, you whisper. If I do
there'll be no way
you can save me. My fingers hurt from grasping
yours. My body seems too great a weight
for anyone to lift. If it wants to fall
that badly, maybe
I ought to let it. I can't
hold on forever, can I?
Yes, you whisper.
The word reaches down into the darkness
where I dangle.
Yes, you can. It is a command.

No stars, no moon.
The sky black. A hole
in the fence, a fistful of dark
in a broken garage window, a radio
left on all night in a neighbor's house,
a book in the bushes,
stiff, rippled pages the rain has already read.
A door swinging on its hinges,
a black car parked across the street,
a man watching us from behind the tinted glass.
Someone wants the whole world dead.
Tunnels under the highway,
a cliff, an abandoned farmhouse,
a television tipped over in its parlor.
Bombs, planets, doom. Supper,
bedtime, night like a wall,
someone on its other side, plotting.
With our whole bodies we listen.

There was a man older than the tallest trees,
the light on the water,
born before fire,
before the great wall had been built we call night.
That's what we thought as boys
and that was why my brother and I one night
started out, determined
to walk till our legs knew where to take us.
Everything we saw
we were intended to see: the bloated rat in the water,
the moss on the sides of trees,
the sun as it pushed through branches
as if it too was searching for something
and couldn't rest till it found it.
There had to be someone
who listened to the world's complaints.
He heard the beetles scratching in the dust,
the gears turn in the clock,
boys tormenting a dog,
bells tolling,
rifles loaded, the opening
of the bomb chute, the fall
of each raindrop, each child beating a fist into his pillow.
He knew the exact count in each prison
camp, each hospital ward,
chronicler of dew as it disappeared into the grass.
This was his punishment for living
so long: to be aware
of the world's griefs,
so much suffering he imagined
he could not bear anymore,
but he was wrong,
there is no conclusion,
no end to sorrow.

Old men stretched out their arms
towards us. The kingdom
under the earth my brother and I had imagined
in our small town on the outskirts
actually existed. We plunged into the world
we thought we'd made up,
lighted cars carrying us under rivers.
Little shops there,
flower stalls, newsstands,
a confectioner's—how comforting
to be a shade, free
of obligations. Ghosts didn't
clean up their rooms,
do homework, write letters to their mother
in the hospital. My brother sent me ahead
into stores. He was too old
to be seen buying spinners and glassies,
though not too old to tuck them
behind a stone bench or into the pillars'
recesses and then grieve
till he found every single one again.
Our pockets grew heavy with the little squeaks
and screeches of glass, violets
and blues the color of night sky,
tiny planets with tinier seas and continents,
meteors and moons, an entire solar system,
galaxies weighing down our pants.

It is time, you say
and draw me to the window.
The city is falling,
the flames are scaling the palace walls.
Look, you say, and because I want to
believe, I see fire
gripping the trellis outside our window,
armed barbarians who turn away
for no one. We climb onto the roof,
work our way down the lattice,
hold on tighter
than the wisteria. That's how we enter Brem,
you by describing it,
I by seeing
what you've imagined. The world is a candle
that has been blown out.
We can almost hear the dark.
It is in the trees. It's right behind us
angled in the briars on the trail we abandon.
It's in the meadow we cross,
the stream, in the bushes we push through
till we're so lost
our legs do the deciding,
it's exhaustion that carries us forward.
The one ahead makes a path
for the one behind to follow.
Your voice is a small clearing
I keep entering.
I call your name, you call mine
as if to remind ourselves who we are,
to warn the night sounds to leave us alone.
Stay close,
Christopher, you say.
I am trying to, Jack.

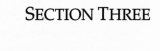

SECTION THREE

PRETEND

One morning I woke to find my brother emptying our room
of everything to do with *pretend*,
rubber noses, stick-on mustaches, fake eyelashes,
evening gowns, long ministerial robes.
He'd taken down the night sky
that filled one whole wall,
an entire solar system
with its outlying galaxies.
He'd already carried most of Brem out to the backyard,
the maps he'd hidden after the flood
high up in hat boxes or stapled to attic beams,
every document we'd inscribed
on the old deeds found in our father's desk,
blueprints of enemy forts, ransom notes,
all our counterintelligence.
He'd had enough
of passwords, palace coups, assassination plots.
There is a real war going on, damn it!
I was eleven, Jack thirteen.
It was time I learned the difference
between reality and make believe,
he said. *See this parchment?*
This chart of the Sea of Galen?
This diagram of the Thavigean Castle?
Now see this match?
He gripped my hand, held it
to the flame, let the fire sting
my fingers. *See?*
That's the difference.
Even then I thought it part of a new game.
A cigarette dangled from the side of Jack's mouth.
He blew rings of smoke into my face.
I remember thinking what a great trick,
my brother can even make fire

do what he wants.
As he held the match to all our heaped-up
riches, our secret documents, our years of labor,
I refused to worry.
The point of our games had always been ruin,
to bring the empire to the edge of extinction.
No one returned from the dead
more often than my brother.
Bored with one world, he'd invent another.
The bonfire was just another stroke of genius.

LOOK DOWN! SEE THOSE ROCKS? THAT'S BREM.

You wanted to play Brem,
your brother teases. *Well, let's play.*
He unbuttons your shirt,
starts to loosen your belt.
The rain has stopped.
The clouds have sailed away,
ships headed somewhere else,
leaving the harbor empty,
dark, the sky
as close as any kingdom the two of you've made up
and as huge. You pull free
from your brother's hands, he lets go
as if you were a doll
that'd just come alive.
For once it's you scaring him.
Still out of breath from the climb up,
you lean out the lighthouse window.
Here's your chance to walk on air.
It may be your last.
And look, there's a path

as if it had always been there
and you'd just now noticed it.
One of those moments
dreamed of so often
when it happens, you almost think you've caused it,
the mist,
moonlight laying down mother of pearl
across it. You'd gone back and forth
between worlds
so many times, there had to be a bridge
and now you are going to cross it
alone if you must.
If you can make the moon appear
you can make the mist solid.
You've got your clothes all the way off now.
It'd be so easy to step onto this path
like walking on atoms
shifting, opalescent
light that looks as if it could hold no one
and yet it is so lovely it seems a failure in you
not to trust your feet to it,
the pull
of every story, places too dark even for the one telling it
to describe.

THESAURUS

Friar's Lantern,
Will o'the Wisp. Fata Morgana.
The boy searches for all the words
for light he can find
as if writing them down
he's drawing in a little of their brilliance.
Effulgent. Resplendent. Splendid.

How can he not shine
in the presence of such weighty bodies,
planets revolving
around the same source, the same imperial
glow? Each one with its own gravity,
its hidden pull.
Phosphorescence. Lambency. Radiance.
He writes a word
and crouches over it,
a small fire he's built out of dry twigs and fanned,
gazes into its flames
till it releases its secret. *Anthelion.*
Parhelion.
Paraselene. Lunar halo. Solar corona.
He doesn't know exactly what they mean.
But it doesn't matter. They are moons
spotted. Darkened.
Light at the mercy of droplets
of water. *Nimbus. Nebula.*
Clouds like great beasts lumbering across a wide plain,
light migrating.
He wants something in this world inexhaustible.
Luminescent.
Incandescent. A language
that appears to have no end
to it, words
spun out, strand
after strand. *Glitter. Glisten.*
Glimmer. Again and again he draws light
out of nothing
it seems.

FIFTEEN

Why do you make me long like this?
the boy asks the breeze on his neck.
Is this how a branch feels extending itself?
How can he describe what it's like
to turn his face to the sun
or see a bird solitary and dark against the sky,
the unfolding complications
of a girl walking, the soft assertion of her pubis,
and suddenly to want more
than he has a right to? Greedy
for so much, yet unsure
of what he wants. Certain only
that this wanting is who he is.
He's received privileged information
the trees have known for years,
the light has hoarded.
He's learned a few phrases
in a foreign language so beautiful
he wants to speak it all the time.

MOWING LAWNS

Because he can't imagine ever being desirable
that's all he wants to be: caressed
by a person of such beauty and grace
even he'll feel beautiful,
graceful. If only he could
spend just one night in that person's arms
he'd never long for anything again.
I'm just a lonely boy, lonely and blue—
he pushes his lawnmower as he sings,
bellows actually.
He likes being attached to noise
so loud and brash
it disturbs the neighbor's Sunday morning sleep,
the minister's sermon.
You wanted me to mow the lawn?
I am mowing the lawn!
The lawnmower travels everywhere with him
like a backup band.
He's Little Anthony and the Imperials,
Buddy Holly and the Crickets,
Gene Vincent—*Just a lonely boy.*
Louder and louder he sings,
pledging himself
to a powerful engine,
its ruthless blades.

Don't expect me tonight.
I am staying over at a friend's.
I don't remember his phone number.
I made up excuses not to come home
so I could bike across town and hide in the shrubbery
and watch the lights go out, office by office,
till it was safe to go inside
my father's building. I'd stolen his spare key.
I was searching for anything incriminating
to tell me what my Dad was really like,
a few used Q-tips with wax on them,
numbers starred on his memo pad,
a condom hid at the back of a drawer.
I rode my father's swivel chair in circles around his desk
and down the long shadowy hall,
taking the same liberties
the dark did, opening offices,
unlocking file cabinets,
the entire building put to bed
except this one floor's
accounting machines, Dictaphones, duplicators,
typewriters covered
like sleek, expensive racehorses
whose reins I seized, a hundred currents restless
in my fists, a hundred wild rivers
harnessed as one. I dialed randomly,
corporation presidents,
a junior senator,
the vice president of a charitable foundation,
everyone who'd trusted my dad with their home numbers.
With each phone call I took off another layer of clothing.
There we were,
CEOs in their pajamas on one end of the line
and I naked on the other.
I left everyone dangling. If I wished

I could shred everyone's files,
pour wax into the word processors.
Taking swallows of my father's private stock of whiskey,
I stood at his window. So what
if someone saw me? Soon
I'd be marching out the front door
and onto the street,
parading up and down before the other factories,
shouting *Down with Capitalism!*
Freedom to the Bankrupt Soul!
Viva to the Entrepreneurs of the Dark!
till the lights came on in every building
and sleepy custodians huddled at windows
watching a sixteen year old boy, pale
and ordinary
as an unlit candle, hold up his hands
and wait for them
to be filled with something more
substantial than the night air.

MOLESTED

Even though he couldn't remember the man's face
he searched for him, went back
to the terminal, waited for the actual bus,
and looked into the eyes of those disembarking
as if having had a nightmare once
he could go back to sleep
and get it right this time, dream it
to another end. Though it'd felt less like dream
and more as if he'd stepped into the world
he and his brother had made up,
cities burning,
boys fighting at the sides of men,

life always at peril. Or had Neander
or Dethrakien climbed from the ruins
of that other world and hunted
for him? He hadn't minded the man's arm falling
over his shoulder, was actually grateful
for this closeness, had begun
to lean into it. He hadn't suspected
that he had anything to offer a man.
The lights had gone on
at the rest stop; all at once the man grew
into more than a voice.
There was blue grit under the man's nails,
his breath was stronger
now that the boy could see him
and not that different from his father's,
like bread gone bad,
like milk left to sit for days.
In the man's eyes, a glare
like that the boy had encountered before
only in movies.
He could see all the way into the man's brain
a fire lit so far back
and so long ago
there was nothing the man could do now
but burn.

Look around you.
There are only two people in this locker room
tough enough to play the game of football,
and one of them is me,
the coach said. *And here is the other.*
And then he pointed in my direction
and I didn't believe him
and then he said my name
and I did. I was so skinny
I'd find the gap in any wall,
fling myself across the fifty, forty, thirty yard line.
It was like darting between cars
in traffic. I leaped
in front of every moving vehicle,
wrapped myself around the ankles
of kids so solid
I could have been tackling trucks.
This was the closest I'd ever come
to the earth: my face
pressed into it. I wore it on my sleeves, inside my shirt,
down my pants, clumps of mud
stuck in my cleats. It made my steps heavy.
We'd lost again. Shut-out.
What was the score? 56 or 42 or 37 to 0?
Red dog!
Red dog! we used to shout on the field and a pass would
drift over us. And then
it was as if we were miles below
looking up,
a nomad tribe watching a tiny plane far above us,
impossibly out of our reach.
A feat of imagination.
A forward pass. One kid seeing the exact spot
where another kid wasn't
and placing the ball precisely in his hands when he was.

No matter how long I played,
it seemed an act of magic—a completion—
and on our team it usually was.
However thoroughly we blocked,
however diligently
we carried the diagrams we'd studied
onto the field, vowed to become the x's
and beat the o's into the earth,
however hard we pushed,
the other team pushed back harder. Whatever we did,
it always seemed to add up to zero.
What is the point of going out onto the field,
the coach shouted,
if you are going to come back losers?
And he kept looking at us
till it was clear he really wanted an answer.
After a game I'd sit with a towel over my lap
and a screwdriver in my hand
and slowly, meticulously
pick the earth out of my cleats
as if small acts like this had to count
for something, unclogging the packed dirt
freeing each spike,
and then wiping it with my towel,
rubbing hard.
as if the point of spikes wasn't really
to gouge an opponent, nor even to clamp
down, grip hold of the earth,
but to shine.

Even as a little boy I was practicing,
pillows pulled down
on top of me, so many
I couldn't breathe,
couldn't push them off, a man's body
like snow caving in,
packed against me, the weight of it
a kind of warmth
pressing me to the ground.
He had pinned back my arms.
would not let me up
till I gave him what he needed,
a kiss. At fifteen,
at sixteen I wanted
to make a door
where no door seemed possible.
One night I finally persuaded my hands,
one brave finger past
what was acceptable
for a young man to do
with himself. I was surprised
by how the body opened,
how it understood. It curled and fastened
to my pain like an old friend
willing to forgive one more hurt
caused it. The muscles tightened
as if to comfort,
as if the bowels were older
than the rest of us,
an invaded city welcoming its conquerors
into what was already ruins
as if they'd known all along
what we were capable of.

CAREER COUNSELING

You can be whatever you set your mind to,
teachers are fond of saying.
Sit down, son,
the college counselor points to a chair,
pulling out brochures like a travel agent.
Where are you headed?
As if no destination is out of the realm of possibility.
He just has to plug it into the computer,
check flights,
book tickets far enough in advance.
You can be whatever you wish,
a boy's father says—meaning
lawyer, teacher, engineer, M.D.,
R.N., C.P.A.—speaking in that voice parents use, knowing
they're being more understanding
than their parents ever were. *Tell me,*
what do you really want to do?

What can the boy say? *I want to be a child*
adopted by vultures. Or a blind girl
who lives in a cave.
Or a hermit who speaks to lizards.
He wants to be washed up,
a castaway searching
for the crew he's been separated from,
shipwrecked on this planet,
marooned in a human body.
Maybe that's why he touches himself so often—
to see if he can feel a fragment
of who he really is, a piece of light
buried in him, broken off from the star
he's spent so much energy trying to get back to.
Maybe that's why he lights matches
and presses the flames into his palms

as if pain holds the answer
folded up in its petals.
Maybe the only way back
is to hurt, to rub against broken glass.

What's on your mind?
asks the doctor. *Don't be afraid. You can tell me
anything.* The boy is thinking
of what he'll have to give up,
what every young man or woman,
serious about making a living, has to:

gazing at leaves, those elegant distractions,
or the creek's long run-on sentences,
its exclamations, its
parentheses, its tireless questions.

What if we made graduation a little more honest,
conducted a ceremony
where every eighteen year old dragged onto the field
all he'd hidden in his closets,
all she'd loved but had no excuse to hold onto?
Final exams would require every student
to write down the idle thoughts
she promised
never to think again. Fire
would grade the papers
and everybody would get the same mark,
flames correcting the notebooks
filled with spaceships or Greek gods
or horses
all a girl had to do was look at, then close her eyes
to feel the power ripping
under her, carrying her into the sky,
imaginary solar systems,
words that excited a boy
just to put on paper:

wastrel, changeling, crucible, relic, galaxy,
maelstrom, cataclysm.

Sit down, son.
Tell me what you want to do with the rest of your life.

PICK-UP GAME

for Christian

A man pulls off the road to watch boys play basketball
for the same reason
he can't keep his eyes off water
moving, its fastbreaks,
a kid sinewy as a wave slipping loose
from the rest of the pack,
water hurtling itself ahead of itself,
flinging free
of entanglements, giving its body over
utterly to the air
right in front of it. The boy glides
all the way up
the arc of his own making, his shot
almost an excuse now
for rising into the sky, the ball
balanced on his fingertips
as if he's carrying something he knows
he must give up. He offers it
as if he's leaving the earth
and has no plans ever to return.

A LONG LINE OF TEACHERS

Trees, how reasonably you send your brood
packing. Look,
even this morning
in what seems a perfect stillness
one lets go
not unlike a child all at once slipping a hand
loose from his parent's
before the parent can think to grip tighter.
He's gone. On the bus
waving. It's my daughter's first year
of teaching. She comes from a long line of shy women
and men who know to listen.
When she claps her hands
her third graders clap theirs
and then they are as quiet as they can be
though they can be quite noisy too
like the leaves
when they want to be,
when there's nothing better to do
than rustle, let the world know
they're there. My daughter
draws the wildest to her side
and puts her to work,
spots a child about to break into tears
and asks him the very question
he knows the answer to,
leans down
so the child is talking only to her,
it's a conversation between the two of them,
for once he's got an adult's undivided attention.
Trees, you have the right idea:
have lots of off-spring
and name none of them so you don't notice
all their little tremblings,
you don't stay attached.

Watching my daughter drive off,
I still sometimes grip the windowsill
as I used to, say little prayers
that her students think her the best teacher in the world,
that she will be loved as she deserves to be loved.
O to be imperturbable,
deeply rooted,
an oak or maple, sycamore or hemlock,
to give birth
over and over and to let go so often
there's nothing to lose.

AIR

Holding a baby in his arms
what father imagines the tortured hair,
paper clip earrings,
a fifteen year old bruising the streets,
moving by a flick of the hips
and by wheels
that any minute might slide out from under
his ankles, a son falling
upwards, a skateboard

tossed into the sky, the feet
catching and holding it high?
Is what my son asks so impossible,
what he hopes from the world,
that it shift its boundaries
and bend for him?
He rides up buildings' sides, glances off
embankments, no surface
holds him for long

as he lets the board slip loose,
abandon him in the air
so then even to his own surprise
he finds his body floating.
He gives up his footing
and gets it again
and again, an arc left in the air,
a faint, silver trail of light
tracked by his ankles,
the wheels under him. He reaches out
and traces it.

What will such a boy amount to,
this son of mine who goes nowhere

except at a slant?

I

What are you looking at?
How do I explain
to the youth stepping out of the waves
and stretching his arms,
flinging the sea off his shoulders
like a cloak he's tired of wearing,
that he is just like the boy in the dream
I thought I'd forgotten
as if a current had carried him here
out of my dreams
and he was shaking their dark waters out of his hair,
the boy king I'd pledged myself to,
had fought side by side with,
had lain down in the night beside
when I was eight, eleven,
thirteen. He was more real
to me than my classmates, my brothers.
I'd told him secrets
you'd trust only to someone you expected to die with
in combat, on the high seas.
I was lying on a battlefield
and he was loosening my shirt, bathing my wounds.
Long before I dreamed of marrying
and having sons,
his fierce eyes moved over my body,
willing it to heal.

II

Hands clasped around my legs,
knees pulled up towards my chest,
face buried between,
I made myself as small as possible,
tried to take my whole body into
my arms, left as little space as I could
for the men kicking me,

uncurling me, twisting my
head back, striking at my throat, the hatchet
blade of hands brought down.
It was a story I told myself
over and over,
after school or lying on my back.
I had to be damaged
so someone could not help but take pity,
a young girl kneeling,
slipping her fingers under my shoulder,
lifting me to drink
water scooped out of flowers.
The honey on the bread she held out to me,
the pillow smelling of cold air
placed behind me,
seemed like gifts not just from her
but from life itself. Her hand brushed
lightly over my ruined body
as if to remind each bruise
there was still tenderness in the world.
And then she was kissing my neck,
my bare arms, my
belly. It was like being hit
by rain, warm
summer rain, the kind that tastes of leaves.
Afterwards even my pores seemed wiser.

III
Do we think they will add up,
all our glances, our yearnings?
The woman on the balcony?
The youth staring out across the water
as if it hurt not to be crossing it,
not to be already started on his journey towards the horizon?
The girl on the ledge,
shadows on her long back,
shadows on the water
cast by the rocks above her?

Seeing her shoulders' slant,
the slope of the rocks she's nestled in,
I want to trace her—
as someone in a museum, against all prohibitions,
might stretch out a hand—
not to seize the sculpture, nor to possess it,
but rather, as if stroking its lines,
he might feel his own body curving,
rising, turned
as smooth.

IV
Too much made of too little?
Of course. That's part of the delight
of sex. The penis's pride.
All at once,
triple its original size.
Gazed at, how often does it not leap up
like a kid in class
rising in his seat, waving, eager to be called on?
In the morning, caressed,
do other men react as I do
still? With astonishment?
As if lost for days
they'd only now been found and can't believe
anyone would search
that patiently
for them? Sex. An act
incredible to a child.
I couldn't imagine doing it,
let alone anyone
having it done to her or to him.
And now my wife lifts herself on top of me,
and as she rocks, she strokes my neck
as if being gentle not just with me
but with the world,

cradling my head
and then pushing down harder.
So much joy I turn away from it trembling,
long for it,
lean towards it,
each day, each ordinary day.

V
You can't be a male and not have heard
other males brag
of conquests, men who have bodies about as lovable
as a refrigerator, who look
like vacuum cleaners
or gooseneck lamps. What artistry
is in their hands?
                    I trip in the dark,
stub my toe. Still shy after thirty years
of marriage, I need someone
who will put up with my
day in and day out moping around the house,
fretting about my failed ambitions or my children's future,
who, even after seeing me hop naked in front of her
holding my injured foot,
                    will still want to
make love.
             How does a man manage to *fuck*
someone he hardly knows? The penis
pushing in again
and again, an instrument attached
to a larger machine
whose controls no one really understands,
an act I still find impossible
to comprehend. It means
touching a person

and touching a person I can do
only after long practice.

VI
If only I could tell you all
I have yearned for, and yet yearn
for it still, each longing a kind of casting off,
weighing anchor,
a voyage that puts our lives at peril,
though the true heroism is to return,
to come back from the adulterous seas,
at first recognized only by the keen nose of a dog,
then welcomed to the table
cleared of everything but one plate, one cup,
and invited
to tell everything that can be told.
It is an old greed. I want to be free
to imagine everything and still imagine
(how can the mind resist its temptations?)
you'd welcome me back,
I could still walk on the beach with you,
visit a museum, go to a movie,
take your hand, be led to the marriage bed,
as if life could be simple, easy
at least with you,
your touch, the gentleness
that weds me still to the world.

RECOVERY

Nothing tastes quite as good
as it does the morning after
the night you decide not to kill yourself:
eggs, hash browns, fried tomatoes, hot cocoa,
a real breakfast
you say in a voice much different

than the one you used just a few hours ago.
Considering the harm you'd intended yourself,
the pills herded together on the table
like a small flock,
a quiet congregation,
the razor blades slid out of their plastic shields,
you guess a little sodium nitrate
won't hurt now. You let the bacon burn
the way you like it,
a whole morning to yourself,
an unexpected bonus
of time to make cocoa, to cut your toast into soldiers
as you used to
for your mother. When she was ill,
you'd heat a little pot of milk on the stove,
mix in a bitter chocolatey powder
that turned sweet as soon as you stirred it,
add two marshmallows
(found at the bottom of an opened box)
and watch them agree, when they hit the water,
to soften—just the way your mother liked them.
You carried everything up on a tray
and she'd pretend to be feeling better.
Later you washed her hair,
tipping her head back,
holding it gently under the water,
your hands fragrant for hours after,
lanolin, yarrow, comfrey, lemon extract,
scents you still return to,
your mother's just washed hair,
the smell of pillows lifted off the windowsill
and placed behind her back,
her sick bed,
as if every journey you will ever take
starts here.

SECTION FOUR

THE JAIL

It looks as if a castle had floated down
into the middle of the village
like one of those magical places that appear once
every hundred years
and then vanish, a fortress casting
medieval shadows over Honda Civics and Toyota Tercels.
At any minute I expect it to lift away
with my class and me in it,
one day we'll be reading poetry
and feel it rise under us.
My students are used to things coming unstuck
from their foundations.
Sometimes I'll catch a man reaching out
and touching a wall
as if to see if it's real.
Maybe it's safer to live in ruins.
No matter how often the men here complain
about the rats, the rotting plaster,
their cramped cells,
the little bit of sky they're allowed,
they keep coming back
almost as if they had meant to
crash the getaway car,
leave their fingerprints behind,
sell to the very person
determined to snap handcuffs on them.

*

Why did it have to be raining?
Why did the car have to run out of gas
at that exact moment?
Man, those fucking cops won't let you alone.
Just when I thought I'd everything under control
everything went wrong.
I was double-crossed. The guards have it in for me.

What could I do?
The motherfuckers were just waiting for me.
What better place than jail
to complain, one more person
dragged down
by fate? Or does a man pull his life down
around him? What men write here
is the story of things pounded by rain,
pulled by currents.

*

You think your dreams are that different
from mine? Mastercard
and I were going to Jamaica.
American Express and I'd scoped a fine woman.
I'd bought my mother the refrigerator
she'd always wanted, the two-door
that opens like casement windows onto an ocean view.
She'd look down and see
all the pastel Tupperware floating before her
prettier than boats in a harbor.
Why, a few more hits
and I could send my son to any college I wanted.

*

Nothing could stop me,
Fly'd say. *Nothing.*
Yeah, Bobby D. would add. *Nothing*
but two cops and a stun gun.
At yard-out the men head straight for the walls
keeping a good distance between them
and all that sudden bright, open space
not to be trusted.
From afar, they look like waves smacking
against a breakwater, tides
lured again to the same unyielding surfaces,

battering a jetty,
sloshing back
under pilings, choppy water
that keeps beating against a quay.

*

As soon as a man's got a fast car
he needs another
even faster, the ideal getaway vehicle
the velocity of dreams.
Ache
orig. ake ME, aken LowG
to smart and MDu akel sorrow
shame IE base agos—what a man feels
rubbing his hand over a new car in a showroom
or thinking about a fix or a woman he's not seen for awhile
or gazing at a candle.
A flame has its own longings.
It keeps aspiring for what's just out of reach
as if this time it will snatch out of the air
what it's meant to grasp
or if not this time
the next. Once again in jail
we are discussing the hunger of the imagination.
What better place?
It looks like a fortress
whose iron gates no one could force his way through,
whose ramparts no one could scale,
take by storm. But let me tell you,
anyone can get in.

We get caught, you don't know me,
that deal
sworn to as soon as the car starts,
the gun's out. *One of us gets unlucky,*
the other gets amnesia. An oath
repeated, hands
laid over hands,
You're my friend, you'll forget me.
                              Donnie looks down
at the fist he's just made. *That's my mistake.*
All my life I've trusted people,
                              He says
as if gazing back over decades,
not a kid nabbed
only eight years ago
with the entire school's milk money.
                              At first he stole just enough
so no one'd notice
and hid it on the way to the nurse.
While everyone else in his class was sweating out fractions
he'd be on her cot fast asleep.
                              I got dimed out then too.
I'd have been all right
if I hadn't started pocketing more
than I could spend by myself.
                              In high school
he had upped the stakes, the band's
trip money. *Shit,*
if they were dumb enough not to lock it up
they deserved to lose it.
                              I'd have gotten away with it
if I hadn't let a couple of kids in
on the fun.
                              Trust no one.

There's no one in the world
who won't rat you out.

And he looks over
at me. For the first time
in our talk, the boy looks right at me.
He does not turn away.
No one, he says.

I mean no one.

TAKING FINAL EXAMS IN JAIL

Kenny X's cut has healed nicely
into a scar. It's what he likes to talk about
after he's done talking about his son.
The white boys don't appreciate that I am a Muslim.
They don't even like the way I sit.
As he goes back to his writing,
his head is cocked to one side.
He's listening to a music they can't hear.
I am too pretty for my own good.

He rubs the same spot on the table
over and over
as if he could feel inside the scarred wood
the atoms' furious energy.

A couple of officers lean against the cafeteria wall
like kids at a streetcorner
waiting for something to happen that hasn't
already. One guard loiters near Kenny's chair.
Then another
and then all of them are gathering around him.
What's that smart-ass up to now,
pretending he doesn't hear us?

The guards stand over him.
Everyone else has let himself be led away
but Kenny X will not be hurried.
He is still working on his assignment.
Even as the guards yank him from his chair
he is signing his name.
He puts his signature on everything he writes.
He does it with a flourish

as if affixing his signature to a document,
an oath
sworn in hope and defiance,
a formal declaration,
words put down at risk and meant to last.

CELL COUNT

Have you noticed,
Jamie starts to say, almost before
he realizes he's opening his mouth,
none of us talks straight
when the women are in class?

Stephen glances up from his science fiction magazine.
Mr. Mac stops coughing.

None of us. We've got too many Porsches
and Jaguars
zooming around this room.
We're too busy spending all those thousands we've got stashed.

Jamie looks up
as if he'd said something he hadn't expected to.

Then Sly nods.
Tiny gives him the *right on* sign,
and even the Ice Man stops twisting his shirt tail
and wheels his chair over
and pounds on the table, *Motherfuckin right!*

And then Jamie's beaming,
that look a kid gets
when he's said something worth an adult
paying attention to, someone
much older than he is
finding him capable, important.

One of those moments that hush the voice,
soften a face
that has tried to look like stone all week,
like iron, a transformation
that even if it doesn't change anything in a man's life
for a few seconds
changes everything.

OUT-OF-THE-BODY TRAVEL

A college criminology class is visiting
so Jesse pushes his wheelchair
up to the cellblock gate, lifts the weight
of his hairy, half-naked body till it's pressing
against the bars. *Hey, Frosh,
too good to shake with an old con?*
and when the young man comes close,
Jesse reaches out and grabs the offered hand
and plunges it down into his already loosened
sweat pants, his grip
tight on the boy's squirming fingers. *Feel this?*

I'd like to shove this hard up your ass.
Two years ago he fell in the prison tunnel,
half his body paralyzed. *I'm cold*
on my right side. That's just one reason
to call me the Ice Man.
Last night Jesse was in Tangiers. He was flying
a plane loaded with angel dust.
He woke on his cell's other side.
Each time it happens, he won't budge till the guards sign
as witnesses. *Look,*
I can't move on my own.
How else do you account for how I got here?
It takes weeks before he'll talk
about his life as a kid.
That bullshit, he'll say.
His mother held down two jobs.
She was putting herself through college.
One evening she was doing algebra at the kitchen table
(Jesse helped her, he was good at figures).
The next morning she was dead.
He gave up his wrestling scholarship,
threw away his calculus book,
and began taking buses
as far as he could get from home in an afternoon,
each day to a new part of town.
He loved clothing stores.
There in their full length mirrors
he stood tall
holding a gun on smartly dressed men
all trembling.
Imagine stepping into the glass,
that perfect getaway.

The foot won't behave.
In an interview, a debate, a state council,
someone's shoe is always tapping
a little subversive beat
on the floor, or is up on its heel
sniffing for danger,
wary, curious
like a startled animal on its hindlegs.

A foot is hard to trap for long,
always ready to escape its shoe
though it loves the sock,
the toes seeking a private darkness there.
Not many pleasures as welcome
as pulling a sock on,
the softness riding up the foot
promising to go further, past the ankle.

In jail the prisoners wear flip-flops
like tourists on the boardwalk,
the feet innocent
of all charges against them.
Did they twist a woman's arm behind her back
or rob a 7-11?
The hands have much to answer for.
But our feet? Who is more oppressed and blind
than these two, tired soldiers?

After he is raped
the young man finds what comfort he can
on his cell bunk, face down, hugging his pillow,
the arch of one foot
pressing against the instep
of the other, trying to console it,
pushing down hard, sliding off,

then returning
to push down harder, the right
like a clumsy hand
massaging the left, two slow-witted
brothers talking in the dark.

JUSTICE

So much of what you'd hoped for,
so much of what you'd worked for
has not come to pass.
So what? How are you any different
from the young man stuffing envelopes
thinking he's dropping tiny revolutionary pebbles
into still water
so the ripples will send out even wider ripples?
The girl leading the charge on the president's office?
The lone woman holding up a sign outside the courthouse?
The new father singing the only song he knows
that will carry his daughter into sleep,
will lift her like a river
ready to bear her where she's meant to go?

You lean across the table
in the prison cafeteria
and plead *Listen,*
won't you listen to what you are saying?
As if saying even the smallest thing
right, even if just
to yourself, could make a quiet place
in a place where nothing is ever quiet,
no door shuts softly.
Your friend back in jail for the fifth time
laughs shyly as if he'd done something so stupid
even he can't believe it.

What can any of us expect? The justice of rain?
Today every little crevice deserving to
brims over with its small portion of trembling
and shines. Even the most ridiculous puddle
turned brilliant, water
in a gutter, clogged
spillage of the most secret drain, sluices
boys have spent a whole day building in a creek,
every tiny crack in a rock that glitters
as if it were the only one the rain had remembered.

So you have worked hard?
So does the light.
It too visits prisons, nursing homes, hospitals,
shelters. Keeps at its labor long after
you've given up. It falls across a woman's face
and she brushes it away
with her tears. Places of justice?
Places of comfort?

Rain to snow
now falling so long it looks like time itself
broken into molecules
and filling the windows. When it stops
it's one huge creature lying across the road,
blocking your door.

In his sleep a man cries out as if drowning,
reaches up a hand even if he knows
there's no hand there
to grasp and if there were
it wouldn't be strong enough, it'd have to
let him sink back
into something too vast to call an ocean,
no voice loud enough
to be heard over its din.

Let no one make light of his terror and tell him
It's okay. Just be quiet,
will you? Give him this much,
his right to grieve,
to keep grieving
long past his allotted time.

THE LEDGERS

Open any page
and there is the scrawled handwriting
of the rain on fallen pillars,
Brem's toppled gates, its scorched ruins
as if we had no other home
but ravaged glory,
as if the point of being alive was to recover
what had been lost,
ledgers all that remained
of our grandfather's import business,
the amber Madeiras he held to the light,
Cognac, Anisette, Amontillado,
Burgundy, Cointreau,
old empires, the taste of their distilled kingdoms
already making us dizzy.
Surely appetite had been created in us
not just so we'd eat and drink
but so we'd imagine a feast
more delectable
than any we'd ever sat down to, chevaliers,
our palaces set in the clouds,
gardens of air where you and I strolled naming
stars, just more outlying territories
for us to administer, the dark

only a provisional government
that could not outlast our empire.
Look, brother, here I am at fifty
still living in its ruins,
keeping its history, Brem, Meregini, Thavigea,
words I refuse to surrender
to the air
lest it corrupt them. I hesitate even now
to trust to paper
lest the page turn our gold lead,
our jewels paste,
and you no prince of Azarth, just another
man getting into his car,
adjusting the rearview mirror,
holding the world diminished there.

A PRAYER TO FAR

Far, blessed, unapproachable father of the universe,
of sun and dung beetle,
catapult and slug, ant and abyss,
streetlight and shadow,
of the dark in a person's arms when he cradles his head
        there,
of the dark in his head when he shuts his eyes,
architect of desert and puddle
(the very one a child chooses,
first the right
and then the left boot stomping down so what remains
of the rain jumps back
in the air, nothing wasted in your world,
no walk home from school,

no hole in the road, even it brimming with sky,
    trees, clouds,
leaping up, water
breaking into pieces), god of splashes
and drips, coughs
and whispers, hummings in a mast's stays, the tireless
prophecies a door makes, swinging on its hinges,
inventor of dusk, of the summer
over before it's begun
and the long, boring afternoon,
designer of screws and bolts, bridge and branch,
sinew and tissue, all things
fastened, all things that fall apart,
author of all the words with which we seek to bless you,
of the entire vocabulary
of water, rivulet and runnel, spigot
and drainpipe, creek
and cascade, millrace and maelstrom, the heavy
polysyllabics
of a waterfall, the tide's blank verse,
every brook coursing down a mountain
like a sentence with no intentions of ending,
every mountain
that looms like a huge, insurmountable paragraph,
every meadow defying precis,
would we ever have spoken
if you had not bolted the door,
hearing us knock, had not withdrawn
deep into these words you've left us?
Would we ever have written our first words down?
All the synonyms for morning light
the birds come up with, every day?
Father, First Word
spoken, Far,
blessed be Thy name.

TRAVEL BROCHURE

There must be a country we could travel to,
a land for those who want to die,
a people there that listen to stories of misery,
stories of suffering,
without being disgusted or impatient
as if they understood what awaits us all,
agony, embarrassments, the body's
dead weight.

On the subway home a man is muttering
to himself. *Sorry.*
Sorry, he says as he sits down. *I don't mean to bother you.*
Two stops later
he is telling you everything that befell him
as a boy, pounding one fist into another
as if it'd just happened a few days ago.
I know it's stupid.
I know I should let go of it but I can't.

A mother discovers in the same week
1) she has cancer
2) her husband has been molesting her teenaged daughter
since the girl was eleven. The two
discoveries get so mixed up in her mind
she thinks she is responsible for both.

He's just come from the gun store, a friend says.
For the first time in his life things make sense.
On the way here he pulled off the road
and loaded the gun
and placed it in his mouth.
How many times had I taken his arm
and led him to a table?
How many times had we sat in his dark car and talked?

Look, let's make a pact. I'll call you
if you call me.
If only there was another country
we could book passage to.
Instead of dying, we could travel,

the girl who looks into the mirror and wonders
how anyone could be that ugly,
the kid who opens his second story window
and imagines stepping out
as if it were as easy as just sneaking out for the night,
the woman who, at a certain corner on the way home,
holds the wheel steady
so she doesn't drive the car straight off the cliff,
the angry man who considers walking into the path
of the most expensive car he can find.
If I am going to die
I might as well do it in style.

If only each of us could bear our guilts,
our griefs,
to a distant kingdom,
to someone who'd be glad to receive them,
who'd open them like packages wrapped just for him.
He'd want to know everything about them.
He'd be grateful for what we'd brought.

Here were gifts
he could not do without.

CONTRABAND

The first guard at the entrance gate,
the second guard who makes me empty my pockets,
the guard just outside the prison library,
each thinks I am smuggling in contraband.
No. No, I have permission,
I say, showing them the note
on top of the sparklers.
Finally we are allowed to turn the classroom dark
and then it is exploding
with little fistfuls
of light. We like the shock
of holding a flame to a metal wand
and pulling from it a great blossom of sparks.
There's a trick to lighting a sparkler,
gripping the match
even as it burns down to the fingers,
hope just at the point of giving up.
And then light
breaking into pieces, so much
we have to shake off the sparks,
keep flinging them away
as if we'd always had such brilliance at our fingertips
and none of us were ordinary
or cruel, none of us
had ever done anything to ruin our lives.
In the darkness we empty every box,
pick up the discards and try them again.
No matter how useless the matches now,
how spent the wands,
still we go on trying to pull out of them
one more burst of light.

AFTERWORD

"Histories depress me. / They leave only pieces of things—a face with no nose, a statue of love / with her arms broken," writes poet Betsy Sholl.

For forty years my brother and I did not speak of Brem, that empire in whose history he had made me believe and in which we had lived as children far more intently than we did in the world outside us and over which we had no control. In school we'd forget and identify the rivers of Thavigea instead of those of South America or name the line of Jeren Far Jeren instead of the Tudor monarchs. During the years my mother was struggling with a mental illness that confounded the whole family, we kept returning to Brem, to the poisonings and strangulations, the endless treaty negotiations and inevitable betrayals that filled our days. Jack created this alternative history by telling it to me, ruling his empire even as he worked to overthrow it, sending plagues across its land and curing them even as he was dying from them. What resilience he had. Over and over he rose from the dead. One of his great joys was to ruin, without warning, all that he had labored over and loved into being; one of my duties was to mourn what he had destroyed. If I begged hard enough, he would let us resurrect and rebuild everything. That was my job: to witness, remember, and believe. And then one day my brother decided the empire would not be allowed to rise again out of its ashes. We were to turn our backs on history as if no queen had been locked in the tower, no city bombed into rubble.

We did not speak of Brem until I began writing this book, forty years later. Was it because we had been embarrassed by this world of make-believe and our hopelessly naive allegiance to it? I suspect we knew that to speak of this world would be to diminish it, to reduce it to fragments, artifacts, "a face with no nose, a statue of love/ with her arms broken," an aberration of childhood, a kid's game. Though for years I had been alluding to Brem in my poetry, never had I dared to enter it directly for such a long period as when I was working on this manuscript. And never had I spoken of it to Jack, invited him to remember. It seemed too much to ask. But when finally I sent him a draft of this manuscript, he responded graciously—as befitting the original Jeren Far Jeren—and I discovered that he still had the old maps, treaties, proclamations written on the backs of our father's galley sheets for his *New Decision Making Tools for Managers*—that my brother still was faithful to the empire.

In this book I have pledged my allegiance once more to Brem; I have tried to recover two brothers' intrepid belief in the possibility of another life besides the one to which we are all sentenced. It is this same faith in the imagination I seek to bring to my work in jail and at the community college where I teach— and my brother brings to his classes and the plays he produces with his students. What we carry to these teaching situations is a shared sense of grief and awe gained from witnessing the spectacle of a beautiful and intelligent woman gone mad and the befuddled attempts of a good man, our father, to come to terms with his wife's brilliant refusal to accept the world's injustices. Living in the midst of great suffering, we came to see pain's mythic dimensions and to respect the agonies of others, those signatures of struggle of which the poet Pamela Perkins-Frederick speaks in her book *Leaf Gnawed to Lace*, the "adversarial stress lines, /their rich and vital power." We learned to regard pain as a transmuting agent.

Our appreciation of the alchemy of pain is what has governed our lives:

> . . . I think of the bird that sometimes sings
> on my garden fence: a finch—small gold bird—
> its song threatening to burst its throat. What
> confines the force of sound—as sound pushes
> against it —makes the song. A fine line—
> the thinnest of skins, a light coat of feathers.

The tension captured here by Joan Aleshire in her poem "Fine Line," describes not just what happens in the act of poetry, but also what occurs in the creation of worlds like the one invented by my brother Jack. What Jack and Brem offered me, above all, was not just a sense of control over what seemed beyond our control, but a belief in beauty—a song fashioned out of the urgencies of our hurt and what confined and shaped these urgencies, the formal and often elegant kingdom of Brem. How could I do justice to what my brother had offered me?

While certain critics may bewail the growing numbers of poets and books of poetry, I find this gathering movement a cause for celebration, a revival of spirit, our one true religion dedicated to the work of the imagination. This book has had the good fortune of benefiting from the counsel of members of this community of faith, poets, editors, and teachers whose generosity has allowed me not just to go into Brem as far as I could but to return from it. To my teacher, Betsy Sholl, this book's midwife, to Helen Lawton Wilson and Pamela Perkins-Frederick who nurtured the poems as they grew, to poets Beverly Foss Stoughton, Joan Aleshire, Herb Perkins-Frederick, George Drew, Sandy Solomon, Cornelius Eady, Roger Weingarten, Jonathan Holden, Charry McGurty Smith, Cheryl Baldi, Elizabeth Raby, Margaret Holley, Elizabeth Young, Steven Riel, and David Wojahn, to wise counselors Robert Fishman and Nicholas Winter, to dedicated editors Sy Safransky and Andrew Snee of *The Sun* and Phil Fried of *The Manhattan Review*, to my patient and generous first teacher, X. J. Kennedy, and, especially, to Ted and Renee Weiss I owe a great debt. Nor would these poems have been possible without the abiding love of my wife Mary Ann and our children, Christian, Nora, and Justin, who, even as they have grown to be adults, have kept the spirit of play. It is a delight to welcome Danielle and Christina into this play and into our family.

"I call you sister. How dare I? / And yet I say it— / Sister— you," Charry McGurty Smith begins her brave book *Something Matters That is Not Being Said* with an invocation to Anna Akhmatova. What I love about poetry is that it draws us together into a community of faith, all of us brothers and sisters. Dearest brother, Jack, you taught me this when you led me into Brem and promised we would be able to return whenever we needed. Isn't that what we love about poetry: we can cross its borders again and again?

For Margaret Thayer

JOSEPH POWELL

Getting Here

JOSEPH POWELL is professor of English at Central Washington University. He has had two collections of poems: *Counting The Change* and *Winter Insomnia*. He lives in Ellensburg, Washington, with his wife and son.

CONTENTS

SECTION ONE

*Everyone's a chasm. You get dizzy
when you look down into it.*
                    —Georg Buchner

FIRST MEMORY

Mine is Catholic before I know
what a Catholic is: like an angel
crossing the street with a child,
memory holds hands with regret.

My pregnant mother squeezes from the car
and takes my hand into a weekday church.
Only a few bent, colorful heads
are scattered among the front pews.
It is a special mass for the pregnant:
the priest's hands, deft as a magician's,
cross candles over their stomachs,
mumbling prayers and nodding, nodding again.
The church is warm and the Latin
a sleepy incantation.
Damp wood, colored lights, life-sized
saints looking out for us.
The thumping of knee-rests, coughing,
sniffs, the blowing of a nose, sliding feet.

When we come out, it is still cold,
breath clouds the slope of stairs—
signals from the angels inside us.
I loosen the button at my throat.
The scarves of the women are pulled
tight around their faces,
their blessed bellies drift like prayer
balloons into the parking lot.

As we sit waiting for the car to warm,
I open a bag of potato chips.
My mother says, "I think I'll have one."
I tell her it's a sin, she can't eat
for an hour after communion.

She says, "Yes. I forgot,"
pulling her hand back.
Then, I see for the first time my own motives
and that invisible angel, escaping.

AT THE UNIVERSITY'S CANCER CENTER

For ten years at Schaake's Pack
my father shot cattle, cut their throats,
skinned and boned them, made sausage.
At lunch, he would come out wearing
a plastic yellow apron, brown rubber boots,
a pack of Lucky Strikes rolled
into his tee-shirt, blood-spatters
on his upper arms, in his hair.
He ate pears out of a Tupperware dish,
his limbs loose, uncontainable,
steam rising from the kill-floor behind him.

I've seen him shoot hogs, cut their throats,
and stand up, blood steaming and curling
around his boots. Or skin a deer,
gently sliding his knife so the skin peeled back,
a clean pearly white. After stroking the steel,
his knife was so sharp hair leapt off his wrist.

Now, head almost hairless,
skin yellowing, sagging like old drapes,
belly swollen, a few teeth missing,
he is already ghostlike,
an image at the far end of all my mirrors.
He is so weak he can only
climb out of the car and into a wheelchair
before puffing and wheezing. I remember

hills we climbed hunting deer,
him waiting for me to catch up,
taking off again as soon as I did
until my lungs burned, my legs wobbled
like his do now. I lift him out of his chair
onto the examination table. He lies back,
looks away as the needle hunts a vein.
He nods to the voice of the doctor
as she explains slowly, as to a child,
her pen assured by the clipboard
that spells out this disease.
He can't take his eyes off the tubes of blood
rolling in her hand like dice.
It is as if the blood his own hands let,
the blood at his feet, in his clothes, his eyes,
came back and each drop of his own
entered the pool at his feet,
its tide rising against him, and he felt its weight
pushing like water at a great depth.
He lies there waiting, listening, one hand
firmly folded across his chest,
as if the needle were a knife.
I feel my own fist tighten,
the powerless strength of my arms,
the hair stand up on my wrist.

1

For twenty years, I never knew
he knew of us. Divorced, he left.
Grandmother's family withdrew.
My father kept in secret touch
but when we finally met him
he was a little man made littler by age,
bald as a turtle, thin skin on bone
with a parchment shine.
He had impish eyes, fixed on
that intoxication of old age, a lone
long draft we take before our rest
by which the world goes round more slowly:
a vacant stare, the luxury of sighs,
a handshake that shakes and shakes.

2

He was our only grandfather—
the other lost to mustard gas
in WWI. Yet knowing him so late
was strange. How to trust a grin
when his silence seemed a curse?
Aches of the heart rarely have reversals
equally as great.

Once while fishing in Park Lake
I watched his knobbed, arthritic
fingers bait the egg-hooks,
the slow, quiet way he played his fish
as if all endings happened too soon.
The human rises to haunt us, anywhere.
As he looked towards the far shore,
his pole-tip would dip into the water.

When we docked, he was the last one out
and stood braced with two canes, rocking
as the boat rocked, said,
"Don't worry, it's steady as a street."

3

Later, half his stomach gone,
then, his right leg above the knee,
he chose his plot, prayers,
casket, a small marble slab.
He spent his last days playing
cribbage with the boys,
feeding chocolate bars to his dog,
nodding in a wheelchair.
Like evening shadows
the elements of each conclusion
rise and stretch beyond themselves.
He stirred his fire with a cane.

After he died, I sent a note
to his wife, apologizing,
saying I was working, a caretaker,
feeding animals, going to graduate school,
and couldn't fly home.
In her deliberate waitress script,
on a scallop-edged notepad
with an Orangetip butterfly
perched near the salutation, she wrote:
Dear Joe.
I was so pleased to hear from you.
Don't feel bad on account you didn't
get to come over. I understand
how those things are. You were
always nice to come and see Guy.
when he was living. He always liked you.
I do to. If that was Guy in your spot
he would have did the same as you did
on account of the horses and animals.

You are lucky to have a good position
So many people out of work.
I have a sore finger, I went to throw
some plastic in the fire place
and it stuck to my finger & burned.
It is hard to write. Lots of love

                                    (Grace)

4
Now, ten years after his death
I see time as a wide street we all
must cross, and it narrows as we go.
More distant from my beginnings
than Grace in her parentheses,
I sometimes stand on a street
watching the way an old woman
slowly climbs a curb
as if it were alive,
or the way a man uses his canes,
to cross an icy avenue.

Blessed by the time to unlearn
each pale in our picket fences,
broken promises of the heart,
I see their crossings as stoic
and all our curbs alive.
What they've lost comes back
to help them cross.

When I read her note again
I feel my finger burn,
for all of us,
and it's hard to write.

ON TAKING A STAGECOACH
FROM ELLENSBURG TO CLE ELUM

We paid for one day to slow down,
for smells to inhabit their histories
as we traveled precincts of air.

We weren't disappointed: our valley
stepped up to our open windows,
stood awhile, then wandered back.
People's yards, caught by frost
and early dark, described our play:
toys still clinging to a win,
or kicked angrily aside,
impatient coats hung on bushes.
There were boxes in garages
waiting to be unpacked,
thoughts that would never dream of waking.
Along the road, dried frogs,
flattened skunks, cans, diapers, pliers . . . .

Because we wanted to step from our lives,
we paid our money for the mules,
for the driver's gee and haw,
the spit of tobacco that announced
a long silence and the lurching
grind of the wheels.
We bumped into the Old West,
a grandparent's springtime story.
Only horses and children stopped
to watch time go clopping by.

I do not believe it is possible to describe or paint the difference between savage and civilized man. It is the difference between a wild and tame animal: and part of the interest in beholding a savage, is the same which would lead every one to desire to see the lion in his desert, the tiger tearing his prey in the jungle, or the rhinoceros wandering over the wild plains of Africa.

—Voyage of the Beagle

People hovered blankly
around the faint lights of themselves
as he looked into the Southern Cross,
wondering about the disordered stars.
From atolls to pelagic insects
caught in the net he towed through the night
his mind buoyed the wreckage of his age
until the unsustained sank, and he
wandered free, making connections, puzzling
them through: silicified trees, brackish worms,
the whole seethe of the secular sea,
its life-spawn budding forth.

He watched with the raptness of a child,
the mind of a man intent on living
up to his name. No thing was too large
or small to be graced with doubt,
even the mountains lifted their sails
and schoonered through the vast lake
of his imagination. His journal
painted them patiently, intricately,
as if waiting to decide what they meant.
Each twist and turn, each node or glint
found the color of a word until even a toenail
asked, What is individual? What history
lingers in an eye, a harsh brow?

His curiosity rippled out like water-rings,
then splashed, brilliantly,
against his shore of facts.

Only the soulless and inanimate
stretched so far back into a plush palm-time
they absorbed a religious awe:
shells spiraling into cloud-swept mountain tops,
infusoria in the deep blue sea,
the "livid flames" of phosphorous . . . .

But women and the *lower orders*
froze in his mind like that horse
in the Andes, kicking atop a column of ice—
perfectly preserved in the very act of falling.
So he marveled at the world's human zoo:
the stink of gauchos living the lean of the land;
the serious hats tipped for a fat, black muleteer
with a goose-egg goiter on her neck;
the endurance of Chilean miners who all day
climbed pole scaffolding with 200 pounds,
fed beans with their daily bread;
the licentiousness of Tahitian girls
immune to the missionary's hell;
the filth of dispossessed kings and cannibals;
the stupidity of Indians naming
trivial features of the land,
land they lived and he left.

With money morality is easy, ethics dovetail.
He sailed back to his country house,
a Wedgwood life, a wife he bored with ants and finches,
ten children kept from the library by servants
until afternoon tea, a *true* English garden and gardeners.
He saw, in poverty, only dim reflections against a wall,
missed the source-light,
the nuances of need.

His hands, held back, missed
the warmth of the human flame
the gauchos fanned with their tipped hats.

A benefactor of truly heroic doubts,
he was, at a silvered old age, a poised man
with a pearl pin stuck at his throat.

SURVIVAL: MONK VARONOFY, 1682

> *He stepped into history like a man caught
> in a photograph behind someone famous.*

In the square a crow hops from one head
to another, then flies to a wooden beam.
The pigs that drug the bodies to the scaffold
root in the pooled blood
of Puskin, Tsikler, & Lukianof,
whose deaths dissolved the strelitz.
Ambassador to Jerusalem,
his journal already sent to Peter,
Varonofy is lost in a daydream of olives, citrus light.
He lets his horse find its own way
over the cobblestones,
drowses until the wind off the river
makes him hide his chin under his coat.
Only this morning he was warned
that pocket-spies had entered the villages
to collect Peter's Beard Tax.
Fresh cuts on his face burn,
and the dead smell off the shore
reminds him of the poor in Jerusalem,
old clothes, knobs of flesh.

He thinks of his journal,
so thoughtless the words blush
at their innocence: *On the way*
to the Cross of God there were two
stairways where the saintly Queene
Helena found three crosses:
two belonging to thieves, one to
Jesus Christ; the first has thirty
steps and its width is three sazens.
Yet he has no bitterness
and the plodding dullness of his horse,
its rising and falling, does not
mark anything inevitable.

On the bridge, a man carrying
a chicken by its feet
walks with a limp and a stick,
raises the bird as they pass,
its low squawk echoes in his mind.
A beggar with lice and bad eyes
sits on the bridge rail
holding a small blue bowl.
The monk looks into the water,
sees himself among the leaves
drifting seaward, his buttons shiny,
his beard already growing.

When the man in orange polyester pants,
thongs in November, red beard and crazy hair,
asked me for money to buy a drink,
swearing he wouldn't dream of buying breakfast,
my hand sifted the change like a bad idea.
Pity is so sudden, bleary,
it loves the pocket it dives into
as much as the coins sliding off the edge
of the hand. He smiled and let smoke
unfurl from his lips, his green mermaid flexed
under a rolled-up sleeve.
He wanted nothing from me, but money.

Thinking we are all earnest oddities
nobody really wants, I gave him that change.
His laugh afterwards rippled, a scornful glee.
We walked our opposite ways, clumsily,
struggling up some imaginary hill.
Generosity loves the hand outstretched,
the poor, poor heart knocking back
the careless hours like shots of booze.
Strange doorways looked on. Alleys reeked
of human waste, dead dead-ends.
Giving small change exacts a change, also small.
My shadow walked through valleys of plate glass
as if reading a long invisible scroll.

BRIDGET BISHOP'S LAST WORDS TO THE JURY

(Salem Witch Trials, 1692)

Last year at the scourging of Obadiah
in Boston Square, a light hovered over his wounds.
With each stroke I could see his spirit
rise and fall like a white bird snared in a net:
his blood was more than blood
and I looked away half in fear, half in pity,
but everywhere in broadening echoes
the sound of the whip was the screams
he wouldn't utter; cat-claws streaked
the sky with red lightning. When I looked

again, a shouting woman was beside me,
her hatred carved the future in her face.
I knew then it was not the ablution
of children we defended by going there,
nor a law that exacts fines for preaching
what we don't want to hear, but an indelible
wrong like the seal Romans pressed
into the foreheads of their slaves,
and so we Obadiah. It was the fear
of moving one more time, rearranging
the looks of icons, and thus our own.

It must be possible to consider
that child clinging to his holy mother
has no more purchase on Himself than the unchurched.
We abolish blame as if it were a law
and play the fool for a grain of truth,
chickens coaxed into the ax.
The world gets as abused by our arguments
as we do. We are but lighted candles
living on the air that shapes our words,
our acts, our spent dreams, and when
someone screams into the dark

in a pretense of courage, the flame
leaps higher as in a devouring breeze.

When Obadiah was cut from the pillory
he fell to earth like something
dropped from heaven.

When my Author reminds me
that the things of this world reveal,
at best, a temporary grandeur,
and the fruits of heaven have no season,
I am ready.

Your eyes no longer perform their service
and are more sorrowful to me than any
sin I committed, alone, or with any of you.
Fear is the whip that welts the truth;
we are but children no water can cure.

I know the larva of evil lies in the human heart,
and mine is as human as yours, but
it is the heat of our own lusts that breaks
it free, that shakes its wings loose
in the light of day. Each time our will trembles,
the wings stretch and stretch until we are
carried on a senseless breeze.

I have seen the devil—he is lank and sneers;
he doesn't wear black, but a suit of scales
that flash like mirrors and make a raspy noise.
You can see yourself in all directions,
at all angles and lights, and you know
that hope lies with choosing the exact one,
the one that's real, that tells the truth
to death's face, the devil's soft words.

I can see the one now, it moves only when I move,
it has a shadow that walks flat on the ground
as if the death that follows us
is a visible darkness, a shape
entering the earth and taking its light with it
to rise radiant later on.
I see it and it sees me.
I'm prepared for your rope
for in your eyes I've been dead a long time.
When heaven opens

we see lightning down here
and at night when we see it most clearly
a ghostly light illumines everything.
If you look into it you'll never be the same:
mountains move, rivers burn, cities disappear.
We are but ashes floating on the wind of a name
and when the last ember blinks out, we fall
into the Great Hand of God. We must pray,
brothers and sisters, that our fears and lusts don't
make us so small we slip between His fingers.

Now, if the court pleases,
I am ready. His Hand waits.

AT THE WRITERS' CONFERENCE: HOTEL NIGHTS

We see ourselves as the only ones awake
among sleepers. High-rise hotels
stand brooding over long faces in windows,
naked bodies sprawled on hundreds of beds
watching the dark get darker.
Sitting in a circle of light,
we pause with half a sentence on our lips—
it has risen off the page, a resurrection
full of promise, or dread.

The line resonates like a pitch pipe,
the past assembles a scene
where we are its element, its absent god.
Scene opens upon scene
as minutes fall off the clock like scales.
We rhapsodize the place we are, or were—
light words rise in their weightless balloons,
flies are armored in iridescence,
the sea is a cadence inventing us
with its broken lines of print.
Nothing can really satisfy.
The stars are retrograde,
gaseous holes like sparks through clothes.
Airport lights are looking for the dead.

Amidst the wreckage of what is,
we sit revising what we've seen:
the cat is winnowed from its wail,
an open onion reeks of sweat.
Yet lusts mosquito the dark everywhere.
The good gods who stand behind the curtain
of a look wrangle with our seedy selves—
the ones that would sneak off to
Nude Dancing, Live Girls, Live Nude Men;
the ones that untether panic
and arm it with nether knives.

Still, art thrills the ache of differences,
its phrases tinkle in the inner ear
like sleighbells or icy wind-tossed trees.
When we finally slide between the sheets
into that clean coolness, soft as myth,
the O of sleepers is a soundless song.

Rambunctious from the zygote,
my son squinches our faces to kiss,
then grinds his lips to ours
like a love-starved movie star.
The faster he's twirled, the better.
There's no ladder too high to climb,
and he kicks off his covers in the cold.
His only fears are bed too early
and the dragon in *Sleeping Beauty*—
its snapping jaws and hissing fire.

His world has plain and simple laws.
An imaginary gun shoots animals
and plants into and out of life.
Trees have knees, tigers talk,
and fish could live as well in air.
Daily, he becomes the things he loves.

Once cautious, middle-aged behaviorists,
we cooed like proud pouter pigeons,
doled out rewards, little blandishments,
but nothing rang the bell in him.
Urge is his only condition.
When he becomes a dog and barks,
crawls around the house biting
the lab, licking our hands,
he's a thoroughly good dog.
All our attempts to pacify the beast,
to talk away the snarl or squirming kick
ended softly in coos and dithering sputters
as if our language failed, or our hearts.

Those creatures of the blood
that race, soar, leap, or creep
cannot be wholly tamed or fed—
of itself an eye can ogle, skin shiver,

a hand curl into a claw. When London burned,
the domesticated pigeons flew
back to their flaming roosts.
It's safety that ensnares us.
They couldn't hear the breathing fire
seething in house after house after house.

LURES

Through an afternoon of keeping
    children from dangers
they couldn't imagine, we sat
    overlooking parked cars,
an asphalt strip. A creek trickled
    through a clear-cut hillside,
scattered as a ransacked grave.
    The steady hiss of water
passed from bank to bank like a secret.
    Between listening
and recollection, without offense,
    the way brothers can,
we floated like leaves here
    and now there,

imagining other lives, vacations
    so good they were impossible.
With the sun in our hands,
    we had the same thought
and drove to the lower Elwah,
    climbed down the dam.
The water was clean, melon-green;
    when it ran, translucent lime.
Evening light scaled the tops of trees.

With only one pole, we took turns spinning
    a spoon by ledges, through the tails of pools.
I sat and watched the water's
    mottled light, rock-reflections:
rushing from recess to recess,
    it was thought itself:
full, then thin, rocky, sand-smooth,
    thudding a log, curving
around boulders in a loud display.

We lost lures, caught no fish.
    Leaving was slower than coming down.
Even the pickup was reluctant.
    Time escaping is heavy
as a spawned-out steelhead waiting
    to begin again. I thought
of those lost lures, hooked like hope
    to a rock. Or ours:
giving it all up, walking out,
    a fist in the air, fishing forever.
That quicksilver dive into the murk.

When we came back, our children laughed
    and ran, eyes bright as spoons.
We played pinochle with our wives
    by candlelight. The cards,
like the future, were ghostly,
    numbers and suits blurred.
Surprised royalty sat up from sarcophagi,
    shapes rose and fell in the candledark.
We bluffed and trumped, made loud claims
    deep into the night.
The game ended in a tie, a lucky snag
    we took to separate beds
where each dreamed a common dream—
    we were loved, happy, rich, and beautiful—
until day dawned and the children saved us all.

SASS THE PALT

Sometimes we say things we don't mean—
no evasion, no hand waving here, here,
or even a limp lie to keep someone happy—
it just happens: while thinking
of one thing another hops in
like a kid into a jump rope. Both ends
are twirling evenly, the game's on,
one line leading to another.

Once it was *Naneum* when *Taneum*
was the canyon lunch was in,
another *cavalry* and *calvary*—
the *l* wanted to change places,
get off that hill and spit with the boys.
In class, I said *breast* for *beast*,
the young Freudians tittered,
the sleepers looked around nervously,
the A's smirked, superior.

I like that kid who can't wait to join in,
timing the twirl, the stumble.
He tickles the swagger, polishes cheeks—
the nicer the rope the better.
Praise to our errors
for they shall inherit our mirth.

AT THE LINCOLN SCHOOL GYM

My son is learning to play basketball.
At seven, his hands are like plates.
When he dribbles, he looks like a chicken
chasing a grasshopper; when he shoots,
he aims for some arc, some momentary ascendancy.

He guards his man when his team has the ball
or thinking of thirst, he runs to the water fountain.
Waiting for his turn to run a drill,
he likes to hug and tickle his teammates,
and I think he is too young for this game.
I make excuses: he's an only child,
we don't have a place to play at home.

As I sit with other parents
in folding chairs long the wall, I realize
I'm watching through my fingers.
What strange shame takes my child
hostage? What disgrace had my mind
outgrown that my heart hadn't?

When other fathers and mothers shout,
I hear my own on the sidelines of my past:
Watch your man, Get open,
Don't just stand there, Don't let 'em do that to you,
Move, move, Pay attention.
In a fit of hearty applause, we cheer
the fine little dribbler, the shooter,
who leaps into the crowd to make his shot.
Even here others pay the wages of happiness.

At halftime, the coach calls a huddle
and the boys circle around on their knees,
their heads bowed, little Buddhists at a temple.
But my son dawdles at the waterfountain,
until seeing them huddled there, he runs over,
stands in the solemn circle of blue shirts.
He cannot help himself, he bends,
takes in his hand the blond head of his friend,
kisses it like a sunlit globe,
then throws up his hands and laughs.
He stands alone, and I want to run out to him,
throw up my hands at all this.
I don't. I sit, eyeing the floor, my back to the wall.

The pre-school is going to the library
in carpools: four to a car.
In the chaos of coats and caps,
loose shoestrings, and things to tell
the teacher, the aides, other parents,
the parking lot is aswirl in bodies—
hands and voices fluttering like seagulls
over a newly plowed field.

My son scoots into the backseat
instructing the boys behind him,
buckles his belt and looks up.
Yet the car is filling with girls
like a bathtub with cold water.
He has plotted his ride through town:
outlaws, firing and screaming
and kicking the seats. He starts to slap
them back, yelling,
"Get out, get out, get out."

I assure him the girls are his friends too,
that we need to share our car.
But he will not be consoled, kicks and screams.
The girls look around as if there's a snake
in the car, perhaps poisonous.
They watch the other cars
pulling away. Buckled in,
they try to console me: we understand,
we used to do that sometimes too.
All the way to the library
they are as sweet as angels.
I talk about the fun of books, stories—
Max and his Wild Things, Pipi Longstocking . . .

When we get out, my son is quiet,
tear-streaked, slow as an apology.
One of the angels touches him on the shoulder
and he swings, missing the top of her head.
She plants a fist in his gut,
and he doubles over with laughter,
swings his hat like a lasso and chases her,
both giggling, into the library, past the "Quiet" sign,
the librarians' fingers bouncing on their lips,
happy to be outlaws, happy to be sailing
toward an island of books
where teachers, fathers, mothers, and librarians
are too slow and old and tame to catch them.

SECTION TWO

O, the regrettings infinite
when the night-possessions flit
through the mind . . .
                    —Thomas Hardy

SNOQUALMIE FALLS

The gray mist rises and touches
the far rocks, soothingly,
as time would if you could see it.
You stand on the ledge
looking down
as if it were your life there
or someone's memory of it
who might save you—
the roar that deafens
into a kind of silence
is everything we can say about it,
is everything that is possible, or not,
and, finally, the water falling
and rising again, somewhere else.

FISHING TILL DARK

We fished in the last half-hour
of light, casting midges and mayflies.
As the insects hatched, they bounced
in the sheer joy of being alive.

After them, some fish made flying leaps,
others sipped or dimpled the surface,
some finned sideways circling, planning,
some skimmed along, missing fly and case.

I thought of the drowned man who yesterday
believed in himself, the river's sweet song;
now, his hands searched among the rocks
for something lost, what went wrong.

I saw a dark blue jacket floating free,
the neck open, imagining a face.
A pallid moon wrinkled on the water,
again when the heron flushed from his hiding place.

His frightened *wroak* made the trees shiver
the way an echo echoes again in our heads.
Black fishbacks arched like cupped hands
calling us in, beyond the easy shallows.

Out of reach they rolled and rolled
until the dark began to subtract everything.
Like water, it filled our clothes, our ears.
An owl called—a deep emptiness, floating.

Cars moved on the high road, earth-bound meteors.
We walked back toward our pickup trucks
talking of bodies, the purchase of decay.
Branches were fingers, rocks were skunks.

We talked louder, laughed, scuffed our shoes.
The moon made long thin hand-shadows.
In the sky's waters, white eyes floated
and the drowned man in us kept looking up.

EAGLES & MOZART ON UPPER PRIEST

On the isthmus between Priest and Upper Priest
where water is clear as air
and slow moss moves like thick hair,
a doe stepped from the underbrush
her legs walking into the river without her.
We could almost believe we were
gliding through a safe sunlit world.

Mozart's *Requiem* erased the engine,
the wilderness crawled up to the edge
of the lake and peered in. Clouds
dove endlessly deep into the water—
our high-minded thoughts flashed,
skippered the surface, then sank.
The sun sat like an orange plug
at the bottom of the lake, warming upwards.

In the middle of Upper Priest,
the engine off, drifting, the music
rose and fell, worked the corners,
then burst into a sorrow so plaintive
it trembled as before forgiveness.
We lay on our backs to watch the musical sky.
Then into our common vision flew an osprey
with a fish, gliding headfirst through clouds.
A screeching cry followed, then its eagle
bald and brilliant. Fierce, intimidating,
it chased the osprey like a hungry counterpoint,
desperate to overwhelm. It screamed and dove,
then rose in ever-tightening circles.
Higher and higher, they climbed, like Mozart
chased by his own greedy demon, his grey stranger.
Outreaching any heights before imaginable,
they both climbed, until they were black flecks,
impossible to tell which was which.
Finally, one bird sailed down on motionless wings.
The white of its tail flashed in a wide arc.

Mozart was still soaring, the instruments
having doubled and redoubled, rising again
out of the ashes, out of the dust,
yet finding their own way back.
The black one with a hooked nose and death
in its eye roamed the hilltops
until the last, exhausted note.

A cold wind came up
and the trees shivered
like the water's white lips.
Grandeur is high and remote: fear-
ridden, accidental, suddenly awesome.
We shivered, too, hugging our clothes,
feeling smaller and smaller.

How strange the world must have seemed to that fish
before it disappeared into the sky.

MR. POPE'S SUNFLOWERS

A weedy garden lines a barbed wire fence,
sprouts small-headed sunflowers,
faces of black eyes staring back at the sun.
From his tin chair he watches
the same few cars go home every night.
In summer, his gray mechanic's uniform
and baseball cap darken with sweat.
His house has shed its paint
and a swayed white horse grazes the yard.

Once I stopped to ask about an Angus cow
on the road—it was almost dusk.
"How the hell should I know?"
The door wheezed shut, then clicked
like an empty gun.

Bitterness loves to be exact,
keep scores, plot retaliations
so intricate no one understands them.
His daughter never stops by.

Early fall mornings, going to work,
I see a kitchen light on
as if the habit of work
were now the work of habit.
A cigarette-line of smoke
from his kitchen chimney
twists toward a few vanishing stars.

The dark can get elaborate.
When I see him in town
hunching along a sidewalk, never
meeting an eye, going his grizzled way,
I think of those sunflowers,
their dark faces leaning through fences,
nodding politely in the evening breeze.

THE RODEO CITY RECYCLER

All day he works the alleys and trash cans
dragging a luggage rack and his right foot
collecting bottles, paper, aluminum cans
for Rodeo City Recycling. He hauls his loot—

one arm jabbing the air like a fighter,
muttering, dodging, wagging his frizzled beard—
as if even the wind had thieving fingers
or the kids who teased him lurked in every yard.

Sometimes, shouting private obscenities
and barren threats, he seems more god than man.
Daily, he faces those inner voices, their lies
and pomp, with more vigor than I could stand.

He snaps his words like a dog bites bees—
risking the sting to stop their menacing buzz.

MIRRORS

1

Across the room, she moved as if alone—
the drink in her fingers, a disembodied hand
that led her on and on, beyond her own
decisions, questions, thoughts of luck denied.
She read his photos on the papered walls,
and seemed to linger on a space too dim
for the time she spent, as if the darkness called
her there, or epitomized herself and him.
She told me once she thought his drowning was
"inspired." She scared me then. I changed the subject.
My sister's phantoms are fed by sneering causes:
caricatures of us her fear selects.
The drink she covets like the warmest hand
is him, or me, or nothing I understand.

2

He thought his photos were an image of
himself: those dark interiors, sublime;
the wan and spectral light, a lyric love
hymn, the nimbus of Tragedy and Time.
He'd shoot an empty room in black and white;
the corner of a window, an asterisk,
a peep-hole sun. Someone's doll or kite
torn and lost were, for him, picturesque.

My sister who never trusted any thought,
especially her own, would dye her hair
or jewel her nose, her life inwrought.
His death was like descending the darkest stairs
and where she ended up was our deepest fear:
down into that underworld, her filmy nowhere.

3

What's a sister to a sister? My self,
before it was identified, was hers,
so that for years our hearts were only half
our own, and yet we fought for blouses, mirrors,
or boys we barely met. This tandem knowing,
for good or ill, was like a skater's tracks
on a pond's new ice: one lagging, one flowing,
then both careening, speeding, spuming flakes.

We finally ended in a snowbank, cold.
I can't now say what most divided us:
my school success, the drugs she bought and sold,
her boyfriends, mine, rites that shaped our disgust.
Though time reshapes us all by inchling moves,
struggles, what troubles love is mostly love.

4

From shade to darker shade, I walk her mind.
What help for those who grimly close us out
to prove some point or recompense unkind?
When we speak, I feel some mirror-light,
my ancient self, come back to haunt me now.
No word is word enough. No touch or look
suffices. My fingers lengthen like a shadow
and grip an empty sleeve, or stop a book.
His funeral gets larger every day:
her eyes have entered his blankest photographs.
She doesn't see mother, father, or me.
A broken doll, she looks at our tears, and laughs.

A ghost between us parts our common air—
immune to love, logic, our hardest prayers.

5

I sometimes think as I look into a mirror
that who we are is never known to others
or us, entirely. We disappear

slowly like a dream that reshapes and recurs
until some ghost of a former face looks back.
How seductive art is—moody film,
or words, or paint—we can't protect or forsake
our lives because some image or fancy whim
might outlive us. How absurd! The mind
is slippery as sin. Its lusts and rapt delusions
are the pigments of fame; regret, its skyline.

The pond my sister skates is not redemption,
the etch-marks of her passing circle back
to scar all mirrors and chill our careering facts.

TESTIMONIES

1 A Discourse On Mules (Suzanne)

My husband was a mule: surefooted in
any kind of danger or steep terrain,
blessed when it came to hard luck, savvy
under the pack, the quirt of a sharp reply.
And stubborn! Stubborn as beestings on a face.

We tried farming but couldn't make it,
so he skinned sheep at this slaughterhouse place
where people wore hardhats, white coats, had digits
for names. He had real regular hours, farmed
at night and weekends. I saw him coming
and going, mostly going. So I started going.
I didn't mean any kind of thing or harm.

I said mule for other reasons, though.
Head down, working the traces, what'd he know
about me or us? When Jim came over some noons
we'd just lay there and talk. Well, mostly talk, soon

as other things were done. Most men have it all wrong.
They work for some golden time in the future,
some little spot of comfort that wouldn't last long
because they don't know what to do with it for sure.

It's like I told Jim: pack a mule too heavy
and nowhere is about as far as you get anyway.
Pack him light, he'll go up or down any old road.
My advice: watch the load, honey, watch the load.

2 On Flying (Jim)

Suzanne used to say she loved me not
because I stood above her loneliness
grinning, leaning on a shovel handle, caught
by the sheen of her red hair, and less
for my grip and wink, but because
I could fly. Could fly any damn thing with wings.
After B-25's in '44 and '5, I loved the sky
more than men or women, more than Friday.
I would tell her things, all kinds of things,
about flying, how loneliness is too heavy for air
and gets left behind like mortgages and laws
that govern earth. And down here, I'm up there
parting the clouds like some Red Sea miracle.
Her husband, Seth, worked against a wall
without any notion of flying, skinning sheep
day in, day out, his life revolving on hooks,
his only music, a knife whisking on a steel.
She didn't take a thing when she jumped his sleep—
clothes and dishes, a rocker, a few old books.
Though I don't think she actually liked the sky
herself, in other ways, she'd happily fly:
rainwalking, what she let herself feel.
Funny, what we keep back because it's "ours"—
our house, our land, our pains, our affections.
When I'm up there, nothing's mine, no power
but blue air, ant-people, the engine's conviction.

When I see the cows spread out against the green,
the star-points of trees, river like a line
thumbed through the landscape, or the wavy sheen
of grass in wind, I know nothing is mine,
and mine alone. Sometimes when I fly over
I tip my wings and she waves her garden hat,
goes back to weeding or watering flowers,
I'm overwhelmed by our smallness, our shadows
thinly soaring over and into earth and that
nothing we do, or say, or think we know
can keep us here another hour, another minute.
Our vapor trails waver, billowy, briefly sunlit.

3 Private Hearts (Emily)

My mother reprimands to make me polite,
to manner my way into the hearts and minds
of people who'd prefer me gone, to ease their spite.
If character were words and smiles, a kind
of systematic hypocrisy we hone
till almost true, maybe I could force my wits
to go along, or bow and scrape, seem to condone.
So much of us is lies we've learned to live with
like boarders who come and go but pay their bills
on time, or credit us with cheap smiles.

To be fair, though, my mother's politeness
is antique, she thinks that others
care what we do. *Care*, a thin dress
of spangles, sequins, and lace. Its colors
are all on show. But what drives the heart
in private is another matter. Another show?
Jim loves to fly and mother loves his love.
How much of it depends on the handsome art
his fear has fashioned? Fear of shadow,
fear of being no one special, of self-love,
of the earth's mice and worms, its rich decay.

Then, thinking long this way, I wonder what
is the end of suspicion, my own dislike?
He looks past me when he looks. I loathe his way
of seeming to listen, the grin he thinks is cute,
or the way he sees the world from the air—saint-like,
above us, immune to earth. My mother left
my dad and found her flying farmer. So what?
I know she slips away to garden. I know
I'll never get inside her complete and deft
escapes, no matter how I wheedle or plot.
I know my father stunk of lanolin,
thought more of his grim duty than death.
Where does thinking lead? What simple sin
against love or life waits upon each breath?
I'm paralyzed by things that must be true.
Love grows indifferent. My face is fat. Undue
emotion is a curse. I side with Sigmund's guess:
with luck our misery's just unhappiness.

4 *Superior Packing Company (Paul)*

Like me, my father worked the sheep.
I always thought his job a cinch.
And the way he worked a knife was something.
As a kid, I'd watch his hand leap
that steel without a slip or flinch
or rasping along a stone like an insect wing
cutting a song out of the night air.
I thought, God, if only I could do that.
He told me to go to college, study,
make something of myself. "An engineer,"
he said, "something clean," and spat
as if to show me just how dirty
his job was. Of course, I knew better.
And like a damn fool worked the fab room
for nine years, boning, trimming fat,
wheeling carts to the rendering trailer.
I hung heads, hearts, livers, or custom

cuts on a tent of hooks. I knew that
I was doomed, too. How little we know
about ourselves or each other! When he died
that summer, crushed by a tractor
that slipped on a hill, my deepest sorrow
was that he never knew how I cried and cried
for him, his crazy life he'd lost long before.
When I was done, I realized I cried for me
too, that prison whose empty doors would hum
of flies, trucks, the mass of milling bleats.
My mother never understood or refused to see
this glooming blood, this paralyzing tedium.
Her life was a flower garden of self-deceit.
My sister, too, hid in clothes and books
and perfected a somber but secure disdain
for everyone or thing you might call human.
She ridicules our loves yet her love-starved looks
go everywhere. Some losses are a broody gain.
When Jim crashed and broke a hand
and nothing else, she was furious.
His engine stalled in the Mt. St. Helen's ash
and he hit the sagebrush, rolled over,
and found himself on Colockum Pass.
She thought he needed a serious crash
to wake him up. Why do the harshly somber
people think they own the simple truth?
And everyone else an addled optimist?
When I went to college and started reading
books she liked, I was escaping my youth.
On this twirling planet, we are all tourists
in flowered shirts and khakis, intent on blending
in—binoculars adangle, safari hats,
snapping twigs, telling others to SHUSH.
We move by happenstance from place to place
and think each move designed by stats
or God. I say slow down, what's the rush?
No one can extend their brief and garish stay—
even sheep bleat to have it another way.

5. Superior Packing Company (Seth)

You know, some days, I feel like Billy the Kid
or Sundance. I just want to hop on my horse
and ride ride ride, right out of this damn town,
and out of this state, out of the whole goddamned
country. I'd find me someplace, some river's source
where nobody's ever been, where trout—those browns
or rainbows—are long and strong as a man's best arm.
I wouldn't take nobody else, just me,
my horse, and enough to get us by. That's all.

I know you think it's foolish, some kid's dream.
For thirty years on the slaughter line, you see,
I skinned those stinking sheep. Three hung and hauled
on a hook past my face every five minutes.
Ten million sheep. I just want time. Nothing in it.

PERVERSITY

Variation on a theme by Poe

There is a knife in every wandering eye—
it comes out of the dark, unexpectedly, even you
aren't safe. There's an anarchy in the brain few
will openly admit. Standing on the high
seacliff: the water crashes up and buckles
back, a dizzy display, rhythmic as blood.
And yours listens: your feet are giddy, your knuckles
white. All space begins to spin where you stood.

A knife, a bullet, a push, a slap, a punch—
they come in waves of violent inclination
with no more motive than a burst of blood.
Our only hope, a willful kind of hunch,
lies in the power of an equally sudden
love, impetuous joy, a restraining hand.

SECTION THREE

*My vital being, do not seek immortal
life; exhaust instead all possibility.*
                                        —Pindar

CANOEING COOPER LAKE

We paddled through snowy crags,
high summer clouds, a circle
of fir trees pointing at us.
My friend, his back to me,
talked about his daily life,
a marriage without definition,
mistakes meant to be kind.
Mine, too, was teetering on the edge
of middle age, another child,
the reticences of exhausted argument.

Free to look at the world
tainted by our own misgivings,
we saw the lake's bottom disappear,
a whole mountain range tremble,
fingers of light grope the dark.
We paddled slowly for the furthest
shore, afternoon shade.
Marriage is a journey, a crossing,
inwardness turned visible—
and all along the way
the unimaginable is pronounced
with ridiculous intensity.
Our words bubble from the rotting murk
and pop into an atmosphere so complex
what can they cling to?
How indefinitely they represent us.

We floated, faceless voices
in a camouflaged canoe, sliding across
jagged surfaces leveled
by the lake. Canada geese
along the far shore barked
their nervousness back at us:
ganders threw out their chests
heads strained forward,

or tilted back, threatening;
geese hissed, slowly stalking, set to fly.
Their brave buffoonery would disappear
only when we'd paddled out of range.
Of course, we couldn't solve our differences—
wound inside us like a mess of lines and hooks.
When we returned to camp, our wives
sat waiting by the shore, but not for us.
We took the children for huckleberries.
As they slid across the mountains, in and out
of clouds, over a dark descent,
our wives were free to find
their own way.

Finally, a gold glow
suffused the air. Millions of insects
glinted at the edge of shade, mountains
crept back to their shadows. Our lives
slowly diminished on their paths of light
as we cooked a cautious dinner in the dark.

WAITING FOR RAIN

At the edge of the desert
there are rainless seasons,
grass so dry it breaks like eggshells.
Dust gets ambitious.
Death rots the water until it thickens,
climbs a tree like a lookout.
The crown seems spellbound
by an infinite absence.
Everything is tense
as a house after an argument.
All energy is conservative,
restrictions amplify, a cicada-buzz.

How sedentary even dreams can become!
Drum-taut, the nerves wait,
cautiously patrol the day:
one chicory blossom grips a dry stalk,
grass smells like the skin of the aged,
a few words spill like seeds.

Desire can be its own fulfillment.

MARIGOLDS

She had said it was never too late,
that even if the ground had frozen
the life below was waiting its season
and would come into full flower in
its appointed time. He doubted when
or if, predicted an endless wait.

She took his hand and squeezed a finger.
They walked Seattle's Myrtle Park.
The Sound slapped concrete blocks
that lined the shore. The abandoned dock
was Cyclone fenced, a dog barked
at a prisoned cat that ate and purred.

He let his arm circle her waist.
Perhaps they'd known each other too long
now to think of themselves as lovers.
She had another man. He transferred
to a distant town, he didn't belong—
perhaps, her feeling wouldn't last.

The looks they sent across a room,
the touches that lingered, shuddered like
fish toward shade, were all

they knew or would allow. A mall,
a restaurant, a dance, were alike:
a furtive guilt ate up the afternoon.

They went on. Days hooked like boxcars,
chuffed, and pulled toward different
destinations. When their wayward tracks
crossed, the time went rolling back
until the present dissolved, was lent
an unreal air, both near and far

at once. Even this evening's walk
was imaginary. A day dream, a stroll
on the avenues of their regret.
The sun stubbornly refused to set,
a windrow of light like marigolds
washed up against their small talk.

The people passing by, alone
or in couples, moved like windswept
paper, cups that swirled in a corner
of strong emotions. If things were
only different, if the cat had kept
an interest after the bird had flown.

They were walking side by side, the trees
stretched out, their thoughts were mottled—
sun then shade, shade then sun;
they walked in front of everyone,
or so it seemed. Wherever they were led,
marigolds only opened in the sea.

HEAT LIGHTNING

1

I sit with a solitude so intimate
memory is a kind of second self.
Snowy peaks step forward, back:
bold, then tenuous as afterthoughts.
Treelines are black rivers
sluicing down gold hills
to pool with the inky dark.

Watching the sky's
equivocation, I could believe
my mistakes, flashing,
dying back into darkness
without me, are shriven and quaint,
and summer's heat lightning
like a prelude to paradise.

2

That mixture of feeling
while watching the light—
the sheer expectant wonder
tinged with a tantalized fear,
an areligious glory the land sustains
in its power and its peace—
sought language for definition.

But sometimes words move beyond me,
more than I meant or felt
as if a siren's song commenced
by a certain swing of syllables.
Maybe in language, its breathing
shapes and sounds, its pennants of feeling,
not solitude, is the second self?

3

All linguaphiles love
the afterglow of the *bon mot*,
the forked dazzle of metaphor,
to lusting for an arrival,
of wanting to go back,
syntax rippling like the skin
of a horse twitching flies.

As I sit watching
the flash & gambol,
the light recede to dark,
the self, too, appears
as a zipper of light
over black rivers,
gold hills,
and pools of ink.

FOOLISH FIRE

This has been the spring of deaths—
people I recognized
by a lock of hair behind a hat,
a laugh across a supermarket aisle,
dated bumperstickers, a dog in a pickup.
It's as if some cosmic electric line
were down and random sparks
left smoldering holes here and here
and here. The more chill
and improbable because the snow
in shade and hollows lingers—
the opposite of upturned earth:
white pools of frozen breath.

Tonight, the northern lights are furred
with city light like some *ignis fatuus*
at the end of sight. There must be hundreds
of sleepless sleepers in that city,
burning away the hours. My own good ghosts tug
at my lifeline, these thoughts that roam
the world for home. The stars waver
just from looking, the sky is full
of small empty spaces
only rapt, vague hopes can fill.

Those who inherited the coldness
of this spring, and never thought blooms
would stay locked in buds forever,
or the mystery of the end was close,
come to me now, shimmering like the light
that crawls over the hills,
and lies there, breathing,
afraid of the day, afraid of sleep.

At the darkest hour, this foolish fire
kindled by my eyes leaps higher and higher.
Night after night that distant forest burns.

How can the dead slaughter sleep?
Fear is a great benefactor that gives you
you, blazoned with fiery details
and the urge to fly freely into the future.
Fear is a great impostor, takes
and makes you the least you: a fist,
an endless prayer, a shuttered room.
Fear is the lion that lopes in the shade
wherever you go, it can purr or roar,
show its teeth, or shake its mangy head,
the breath behind these very words.

When the dead come back—
uncle, neighbor, friends, acquaintances—

I try to hold their lives,
moments I didn't know,
and those I did, like light:
the aurora borealis, fox fire, will-o'-the-wisps,
a city throwing itself over a mountain.

THE NEWS OF STAFFORD'S LAST DAY

The small headline announcing his dying
hit like a frost warning,
a threat to all the warmth
the world might offer a darkening time.
It was like climbing lightless stairs
and finding the handrail gone.

I kept thinking of his last room,
its light resting on the windowpanes,
dust motes that would never again
recommend anyone or anything:
his mother's broom, a lost brother.

Few men live well enough to be a credit
to their precepts. His public privacies
allowed our privacies to take public chances,
to live as wrongly as everyone
but with a decent amends.

Twice he came to our small town
to read his poems, talk his eager creed.
At the last one, he coughed & coughed,
his face red as a raspberry, eyes glistening,
voice shrinking into a whisper.
In front of all our embarrassments
he wheezed: "Don't worry. It doesn't hurt."

After the murders, the high-toned
failures, the moral outrage
over a pitcher's bad game, verbs too big
for their headlines, in a tiny corner
on a back page reserved for the truly
newsless, they announced his last day.
I still hear his voice
wheeze, then rise like a leaf
stricken but aloft on the wind
of all our doomed but hopeful breathing,
sail confidently back
to the waiting earth.

FINE DISTRACTIONS

> . . .the sea's heart—that fertile entity like
> the mind in its swarming and grotesque life.
> —Loren Eiseley

1

This morning sleep hung on and on—
my dream upholstered the room:
in my grandmother's house
a dead man walked through the door,
his long-dead voice surprising no one.
Everyone's hair was still like his.
Finally, his story invented another life:
a parrot spinning on its branch like a revolver,
a leopard slinking along a dappled floor.
I awoke, astonished by my own green wallpaper.

I was neither myself nor him,
merely a roving eye, a body made of light.

2
Some days, you work on me this way.
From verge to verge, I move
in a fine distraction: your
perfume is a staircase,
a soft ascent; your fluent
hand over my back, along a thigh
obliterates my brain's toy empires.
My head's a flower in your sway.

3
If the mind were an ocean,
the body would be its lonely bed—
sleep, love, their best embrace.

ON TANAGERS

I have seen you in the woods, here
now there, the shadows compatriot
with your modesty.
As between forest and plain,
you live on the edge of perception.

In our every wish, a piece of you,
abstracted from you, rises from insects,
the bruised fruit, the spiked seed,
an essence that busies the canopy with light
so varied and splendid, the mind is dumbstruck,
an electric delight. Every poem wishes
to be you, ignited by a ray of light
among green shadows and tall trees;
every lover wants to see you
in the mind and body of another;
every song stretches its fingers
to touch your humble glamour.

Your beauty is a shy mirth
as if you wore the dexterous range of color—
apricot and raspberry, green on greens,
violets, streaks of white and amber—
not to impress or cajole, not to bless,
but to bemuse us so we might
relish the private joy of possibility.

THE ART OF COOKING

I once thought good cooks
   like morticians
made death sweet, delicious—
   they swaddled it,
dressed it up in aspic,
   or sugar skirts.
It was irreverent play,
   the way a dog
flings a mouse into the sky,
   shakes it, pats it,
then trots off, nosing the air.

Then I married a good cook.
   Watching her knead
the dough, roll it,
   wrestle with it,
turning and pulling and patting,
   I recognized
that face, the fixed frown
   that ended fights,
saw how personally
   the hands knew
how they struggled to invent—
   pulp from the prickly pear,

weeds fashioned into herbs, breads,
 nuts leached and mortared—
all to serve the simplest needs.

 Our kitchen
looks like an alchemist's study:
 jars of fennel,
fenugreek, feverfew—labeled, alphabetical;
 teetering piles of books;
crocks of ladles, tongs, mallets, spoons;
 herbs drying on walls.

She praises the dignity of paella
 and supple colors
sliced in circles, innuendoes
 placed in space,
meant to disappear honestly, slowly,
 in a delicious unbecoming.

She believes in the tongue's honor,
 perishable gestures,
is suspicious of a word's intent
 the way an *I*
insinuates itself across the page
 or into an inner ear.
Sometimes I wish all these words would
 disappear, one savory
bite after another, the last line
 a fine dessert.
Although I know some have husks, poisons,
 or grow as we eat them,
those words I ate, every last syllable,
 were delicious
for years and years. All our endings
 begin with a clatter of dishes,
brief grace, a little steam rising, dissolving.

THE GRASS AT HOLY CROSS CEMETERY

(Emily Wickwire 1978-1994)

After Emily's funeral
in a town too small for death,
the children came all summer with wreaths
and flowers and their starved, bottomless looks.
It was as if they saw for the first time
that black spot on their hands
passed to them by a dying man,
couldn't believe it was their hands,
the depth of sorrow, how it gnaws
on itself, widens and deepens,
how endless its vistas, steep its chasms.

No one outside their group—
not the minister who praised her smile,
her beauty, her good and giving heart,
and entrusted her to God's mysterious mercy;
not their mothers and fathers who had welcomed her
into their homes, talked over dinner, drove them
to swim meets and dances, helped paint pep rally signs;
not those relatives from out of town
who touched her pink coffin and left;
not the townspeople who wrote letters to the editor
expressing their sorrow, the care of Jesus—
no one had ever loved her as they did.

So they had only each other,
sat in groups of three or four.
Some would come alone, afterwards,
bowing their heads, looking at the grass,
their fingers moving through it, twisting,
pulling. They chewed it, broke it apart,
watched it lie down, rise up slowly.
Their fingers were stained with it,
they wore it on their jeans and shoes and elbows.
It clung to them like the memory of her perfume.

Stained and bent, they hugged each other
as if they would never let go
and the grass were beginning to teach them
about the world of the spirit, the lives
they walked through getting here.

AFTERWORD

If philosophy is about the nature of our being, then poetry is about the nature of our well-being. I believe that if more people read poetry, they could be better people. The more we read about the human heart and mind, the more we understand the predicament we are all in. Cynthia Ozick wrote in an essay that "metaphor is the herald of human pity"; I would like to believe that this is true.

Because of its small audience, poetry, more than any other art, has to mean something to the poet. Publishing a book of poetry can be a little like throwing a party no one attends. For the poet, the process of examining what we feel and think, as well as what others think and feel, should lead naturally to a more deliberate, inspired, and emphatic life.

In any kind of writing, I value honest directness, economy, and apt figurative language. Alfred Jarry, a French poet, said that "simplicity does not have to be simple; rather, complexity drawn taut and synthesized." Although the assumption that complexity can be expressed simply is almost a given in physics and mathematics, we tend to forget it when discussing the virtues of good writing. Even though I admire elegant simplicity, I don't achieve it often, but I revise with this goal in mind. I also think poems should retain a little mystery, not because the writer is mysterious or the language is confusing, but because we are all complex and mysterious. Most acts and reactions are so layered with odd motives, bull-headed quirks, chemical urges, or high-minded resolves that easy answers only lead to stereotypes. The best poems seem to hum with the excitement of being alive.

FADHIL AL-AZZAWI

In Every Well
a Joseph is Weeping

*Translated
from the Arabic
by Khaled Mattawa*

FADHIL AL-AZZAWI was born in 1940 in Kirkuk in northern Iraq. He studied English Literature at Baghdad University, then went on to Leipzig University in Germany, receiving a doctorate in journalism. He edited literary magazines and newspapers in Iraq and elsewhere. His works include six volumes of poetry, six novels, one volume of short stories, one volume of criticism, and numerous works of translation from German and English. In 1977, he left Iraq for Germany. The poems in this translation come from his newest books, *At the End of All Journeys*, 1993, and *A Man Throwing Stones Into A Well*, 1990.

KHALED MATTAWA is the author of a book of poems, *Ismailia Eclipse*, and the translator of *The Questions and Their Retinue: Selected Poems* of Hatif Janabi. An assistant professor of English at California State University, Northridge, he was awarded the Alfred Hodder Fellowship at Princeton University for 1995-96.

CONTENTS

BROTHERLINESS

In a tower
climbing the sky
inside a closed glass room
a skeleton sat very close to me
and put its hand on my shoulder, mumbling:
"You are my brother,"
then gave me a butterfly
heading for the flame.

Descending in the dark
tripping on the steps
the world came to me and put its heart in my palm.
It burned my fingers
like an ember
wrapped in ash
and blotted with human blood.

A permanent truce
between man and what came before him.
A permanent truce
between the wind and the tree.

Put out the fire,
let the butterfly return to its flower.

INTERSECTIONS

The ship that did not arrive
The house that wasn't built
The road not traveled
The letter that did not come
The well not dug
The tree not planted
The cigarette not smoked
The coffee not drunk
The death that did not come
The life that did not begin

In every ship there is a smuggled traveler
In every house lost memories
On every road a returning caravan
In every letter a forgotten sentence
In every well a Joseph is weeping
In every tree a forbidden apple
In every cigarette a Red Indian
In every cup of coffee there's bitterness
In every death a drunken angel
In every life there are mourners waiting

At the border station
there's an officer who knows you well.
Shake his hand or smile at him
then pass by quietly.

IN CAPTIVITY

From an old folk song,
a couple of slaves fell on the roof
of our house in Baghdad.
They were tied with a rope,
back to back,
wearing torn white clothes
and weeping.

I believe they were waiting for a ship, sailed by pirates.
I believe they were staring at a horizon of trees.
I believe they were thinking of a distant island.

When I climbed to them and released them from the rope
they lit up in flames in my hands
and turned to ash.

IN THE COURT OF HONOR

In one of my incomplete poems
a sentence challenged another
and slapped it with its glove—
inviting it to a duel
in the Court of Honor.

At the end of the fight,
and as happens often,
one of my sentences was dead
and the other bleeding on the page.
I did not want
to get involved in the maze of criminal investigations
between question and answer,
and so preferring to wash my hands
of their blood
I threw away the whole poem.

9 AL-AZZAWI

OUT OF HABIT

In the elevator of the Europe Center tower in Berlin—
and as I was going to see a famous Greek dentist
who lives on the 15th floor
to pull the last of my molars—
a Bedouin clung to my coattails.
He had left his horse grazing
on the artificial grass
and started to cry out loudly:
"I am Al-Mutanabbi,
Save me."
The poor man was writhing from hunger
after he'd spent all his money
on the prostitutes who stand in the evening
lined up on the sidewalks of Kudamm
in front of the billboards.
I suggested that I guide him to an Orientalist
who'd memorized all his poems—cover to cover—
to lend him money.
But he refused
and asked that I take him to the king of the Germans
so that he might praise him in a poem as he'd done
in every foreign country he visited.
So I led him
on foot
to a German museum filled with kings
and left him there
and fled with my skin . . .

AN OLD CONTINENT

Happy memories of a sun
in a missing neighborhood in a city
where rivers run below
and where a child climbs down a tree,
the roof of which is the sky,
and alone rebuilds his shattered soul,
in his hands a bulbul he'd caught
a long time ago from a continent
the sea may have submerged.

In that old hall
where kings give away their silver to ants
the game of forgetting is time.

We have always searched for fire
in the intersections of point zero.

Mountains of ash
and a spring
where sinners bathe,
mountains without end
and fire again.

The rains
have ruined our fruit
and spiders
have built their civilization
in front of caves.

Our guide
is madness in the forest
as we slide
to the last tributary
of the river.

As I was traveling by bus
between this life and the hereafter
the angel Gabriel hopped in—
a hat on his head,
its rim sloping over his forehead—
wearing a wide coat
and looking like one of the fugitives
on the sidewalks of Bahnhof Zoo.
He got in without buying a ticket
and sat on the seat beside me
pretending to look through the window
like an American tourist.
On the road he poked me in the waist
and began reciting his new holy verses
into a tape recorder he held in his hand.
His monotonous voice nauseated me
and I rose to escape.
But he caught up with me and threw me back into my seat.
He pressed his gun against my chest
and said threatening:
"Next time, O prophet, I will shoot.
Now recite. Recite
in the name of thy God who created thee."

SILENT PARADE

Placing my hands in my torn pockets,
walking down the street,
I saw them watching me suspiciously
from behind the glass panes of stores and cafés.
They walked out quickly and followed me.

I deliberately stopped to light a cigarette
and turned around, like someone giving his back
    to the wind,
to catch a glimpse of this silent parade:
theives, kings, murderers, prophets, poets
jumped out of everywhere
to walk behind me
and wait for my signal.

I shook my head in surprise
and walked on whistling
the tune of a popular song,
pretending I was playing a part in a film
and that all I have to do is to walk on forever
to the bitter end.

THE MONSTER

Among the trees a road turns around itself.
I walk it in snow, alone at night.
From a distance I hear the sounds of trains
standing and howling.
From them a worker gets out returning from a dance party
accompanied by a soldier who may leave her at dawn
and disappear.

Or on these trains a man
who had forgotten his address in a bar
may climb.
From the woods I return alone shivering in the cold.
I open a closed door.
I switch on the light. I switch off the light.
On the corner of my bed
I notice a monster
sitting like a coquettish cat
looking me in the eye.
I hold him by the hands and throw him in the snow
like a dead crow
and begin to think of the trees.

MAGICIAN'S HAT

I take off my hat
and place it on the table in front of me.
I fill it with all I have in my pockets:
keys, pack of cigarettes, wallet,
handkerchief, address book.
I wait for a woman to come out of the hat,
a woman who will rest her head on my chest
and say "I love you."
I wait for a star to come riding a wave
and maybe a small stream
gushing in springtime.
(But nothing happens,
nothing ever happens).
Despairing,
I pin dawn to the head of a spear
and surrender it to the birds.

BETRAYAL

To Omar Bin Abi Rabi'a

Once
Hind Bint Al-Haritha visited me
in my room.
She took off her clothes and said:
"Do you find me
the way Omar Bin Abi Rabi'a praised me?"
I said: "Let's forget about him, girl!"
She bent toward me
and kissed my mouth.
Then she lay on the bed and said:
"Come hither!"
After a night of hell
she wore her short florid dress
at dawn
and left, returning to her family compound.
She asked that I send you her greetings
if I meet you
one day on the street.

HOW TO WRITE A MAGICAL POEM

There's nothing easier than writing a magical poem
if you have strong nerves
and good intentions, at least.
It's not that difficult, I assure you.
Take a rope and tie it to a cloud
and leave one end of it dangling.
Like a child, climb the rope to the end
then throw it back to us
and let us try to find you—in vain—
in every poem.

No one's in the house, Robinson Crusoe. They have heard the call and slinked, one after the other, to the dark tunnel trudging through the cold water stream, muffling their weak voices, carrying their lanterns in their hands, searching for their shadows on the walls that have bent with time. They all panicked and left their provisions to the rats and hid in the crevices afraid of getting wet.

No one's in the house waiting for you, Robinson Crusoe. The cloud you left there the wind has sunk it all the way down to the mountains. On the sands saturated with the smell of tar, the thieves left their marks promising to come again. And the dead rose to their coffins even before we drank a toast to their last farewell. There's no guarantee for you, sitting on the rock, shoeless, dangling your feet in the calm sea, watching the horizon with your friend's binoculars, the one who was eaten by a whale. Your consolation is the sun on the heads of the trees in the middle of the morning, and your inheritance is this gulf congested with turtles and fish building their kingdoms beside your hut. The comet at night and tropical rain at noon. And if you're lucky maybe a mermaid will come to you out of the sea so that she may spend your sweetest days with you.

No one in the house talks about you, Robinson Crusoe. Everyone abandoned you when you became the witness and the victim. I leave you to your fate which you earned, taken as you were with our latest dreams and delusions. So remain on your island, forgetting and forgotten, and remember that we all loved you with sincerity.

THE GENERAL'S LAST NIGHT

There, way up in the heights,
I saw him standing, resting his elbow on the bar,
gabbing with a general who'd just returned from battle.
—That's not true, you can't believe all that's said.
—There are other ways.
    Just look at the maps.
His back was to the mirror
where there was an elm tree in the desert
and below it a horse whinnying.
That night
while the rains poured
I heard a train drag itself in the dark
and many generals got out of it.
At the end of that night
I saw him get into the last car
of that long train.
He was dead, had been so
forever.

FAREWELL

Alone he walks toward the scaffold.
His hands behind him, seven rifles pointed at his back.
He thought of who will weep silently over him.
He dreamt of the sun after he is gone, and the birds
and the river
and the . . . and the . . .
And he looked at a date palm the wind penetrated
and shook. He saw a cloud:—"Maybe it will rain after
    my death."
He noticed a narcissus hiding among the grass behind
    the fence:—

"A man will pick it and give it to a happy girl
who will leave it behind on a bench when she leaves
      the park."
He stretched his eyes to dawn breaking. He was alone.
When he climbed the wooden stairs,
a dove sleeping on the scaffold
was startled
and flew away.

ON A DISTANT ISLAND

It's best that you wear a handsome suit
when you go out at night to the street,
for thieves will follow you
if you happen to have a bundle of keys in you pocket
and if your heart is empty of envy.

Good: Here is your bolted box,
your box which might have a treasure inside,
your froth-covered box which the sea dragged
one morning to the shore
from a ship that sank a thousand years ago.

Ages pass over the rocks. The sounds of distant waves
and trees moaning in forests. Fish and caves.
Fish and checkpoints tracking smugglers
returning with loot.

I used to know the captain. A grave man from a
      distant island.
He left and did not return. He left us with his memories.
It's not important that we talk about him after
      what happened.
That's his box there, let's both carry it to the house

and bury it under a tree
until next spring
as long as we have a lot of time.
And if we get enough money
we'll buy a new ship
and return with it to him.

I know he's still waiting for us there
looking at the horizon through his binoculars.

ON A NIGHT IN WINTER

On the night the three kings
came from the east,
and headed toward the mountains,
carrying their gifts
and following the star that led them to Bethlehem,
I saw the Pope searching for them and looking worried
in his Rolls Royce.
On his head he wore his old crown.

Returning home
I heard the child crying in the grotto,
and the time was winter.

ALWAYS

There's always someone waiting for you
lying on his back
on the grass in a park.

There's always a clean sky
overhead
and a helicopter
soars over the woods
where a soldier and a woman
cross
a pond filled with fish.

Always a brook and trees. Always
a brook and an owl.

A horse running by in the morning
and a man dying in a park.

ARRIVING LATE

To a man who died a thousand years ago

If I was late in meeting you
it's because I lost all my travel papers
which I bought from God.
Worst of all was that all the buses passing by
were filled with wicked travelers
carrying knives in their pockets
hoping to get me.
So, my friend, I had no choice; nothing was left
but this long highway
which led me
upwards to the devil

waiting for me at the first station,
in his hand his three-headed lance.

I was in hell
where there are nuclear-powered ovens
and snakes as long as the distance
between the heavens and the earth,
humans tied in chains,
and a filled cup of poison
that you'd have to drink in one gulp
like a Russian drunkard after a speech about friendship.
I was in heaven
where there are remote public resorts
crowded with prophets and saints
sitting on stone benches
and reading detective novels
where everything happens in the hereafter.

I remember an angel who took me to his house
and gave me coffee with milk.
Then I lost my way in the forest
and the wolves clawed me.

I know I was late in getting to you.
Nonetheless, there's nothing urgent—
even if you waited another thousand years—
because everything will always begin again
like a play performed everyday
and we have all eternity to see it.

A MAN IN MEMORY

for Jamal S.

For many years
he kept panting behind me
like a deranged dog
from protest to protest
from trial to trial
from alley to alley
café to café.
In the morning, on my way to college,
I used to see him standing in front of the black gate
smoking and leaning on his bicycle.
And at noon, heading to the students club,
I noticed him sitting on the dirt platform
of the northbound train
holding an egg sandwich, devouring it,
and looking for me with his deep-set eyes.
He knew no one except me
and so he recorded my name
in every report he gave to the police
in Aiwadiya.
After many years
(and I had forgotten him by then)
they took me in once
to stand before a military court
whose members were suffering from boredom
and who had pulled out some ragged papers—
papers the mice had been feeding on—
in order to pass the time.
They brought him to witness against me
as he had always done.
But as soon as he saw me guarded by soldiers in the hall
he hurried toward me and greeted me like a lost brother.
They had thrown him out on the street
after he'd gotten old and was out of strength.
He told me: "No one needs me
        and I have always served them."

When they called his name, he entered stumbling
    from alcohol.
He must have drunk a bottle of araq beforehand.
He put his hand on the Quran
and swore that I was the noblest man he'd ever met
    in his life
and that all he'd said about me in the past
was a lie and outright slander.
So the court forgave me
the many transgressions I did not commit
and declared me a good citizen
in the annals of the state.

On the way to the city
we rode the same bus and he sat beside me
and asked me shyly
to reward him with a bottle of araq.
I bought him a whole box
and he carried it and left.
After two or three months
he came to my office drunk.
He dropped his head and began to cry,
and talked about his young wife
who was cheating on him
with his secret friends
whenever he went to the bar at night.

Every two or three months
he came to me
to give him enough money to keep him drunk for a week,
then he'd leave tripping on his own steps.
So many months passed without him coming
that I thought him dead.
But then he showed up one last time
and sat in a chair in front of my desk
and apologized for his whole life.
He was in the highest degree of sobriety.
He said: "Give me two dinars and you won't see me

after today;
I will disappear from your life forever."
When he got up he shook my hand very warmly,
    unlike him,
as if he was a friend traveling to a distant city.

After a few days I learned that he slit his own throat
with a shaving razor.

ON THE EVENINGS OF VICTORY

To Napoleon Bonaparte

O Conqueror, O Conqueror
what did you do on the evenings of your victory?
I think you changed your dirty shirt
for a clean, ironed one.
I think you went to the bathroom and shaved your chin
while the soldiers washed your sword.
I believe you sat with your generals
on cushy sofas
and guffawed listening to a joke
told by a clown
wearing a helmet on his head.
I believe you left
and started pacing the room,
your mind crowded with rapacious emotions.
There's always something missing
but you don't know it yet.
Only defeat knows it
and you were not defeated.
On the evenings of your victories
I believe you stayed up all night
and slept through next day.

Victory knows sleep
and you were victorious.
I think you replayed the battle in your head
and killed thousands more,
thousands who luckily did not die.

Oh God, what mistakes you made!
You could have lost the battle
if the enemy hadn't revealed their rear flank,
if a shell hadn't fallen on their artillery and destroyed it,
if a bullet hadn't hit their leader and killed him,
if his horse hadn't bolted and fallen in a ditch,
if the sun hadn't been in his soldiers' eyes
and caused them to get lost in the fields.

In every victory there is
postponed defeat.

O Conqueror! O Conqueror!
on the evenings of your victories
you will know how to weep.

SONG OF MYSELF

When I reached ten
I said to myself: Everything will be all right, Fadhil,
as long as there are seasons turning,
as long as winter surprises you with its rain
and spring with its wild flowers
and summer with its blazing August
and autumn with its profound sadness,
as long as you sit on the front step of your family home
    in Kirkuk
watching black clouds in a red sky,
fleeing, followed by horses and elephants.
I said: When you get to be twenty
you'll go to Musallah garden
and stroll in the afternoon at the foot of Said Gezi hill,
and in the evening you will sit at a café near Qaisaria
and stare at the small storks
perched on top of Naqshali Manara Si tower
chirping for you.

And when I got to be twenty
I wasn't in a park or a café
but in Baghdad prison
guarded by policemen from the country who woke us up
    every morning
to run ahead of their clubs with which they flogged us
forcing us to squat in "the grid"
in long lines
and to be counted like sheep inspected by the butcher
before being led to the slaughter house.
I said then: Everything will be all right, Fadhil,
as long as all of life is ahead of you
and your heart is filled with hopes,
and when you're thirty
you'll return to your family
and your missing friends will come to you

from their new places of refuge
to tell you about cities on the Tropic of Capricorn
and others on the Pole.

When I reached thirty
I myself was in exile.
I said: Everything will be all right, Fadhil.
When you get to be forty
you will return to your bankrupt poet friends
who will wait for you in the evenings
sitting on benches on the sidewalk
sipping tea from Café Majid.
You'll get drunk together night after night
at the Adlia Club
cussing out the government
and loafing about on the empty streets
until dawn.

And when I reached forty
I saw them all escaping, one after another,
with fake passports
or crossing borders
with smugglers leading their donkeys
through dangerous mountainous terrains.
And we got drunk together
once here and once there
in Berlin or Cyprus
or London or Paris
and sometimes
in hell.
I said: Everything will be all right, Fadhil,
as long as your memories are with you, at least.

When you get to be fifty
you'll return to your forgotten tree
to water it from your palms,
and to rebuild your house

which the wood worm ate,
and to your books, left behind in cardboard boxes,
to read them again.

And when I reached fifty
I saw our old tree cut down with an axe
and our house infested with rats
and my books thrown in a well.

And now what will you say to yourself, Fadhil,
now that you've burned all the ships you left behind?
Oh, I don't want to say anything,
I won't say anything.
Leave me alone, damn it!
I've reached the end
in one second,
and learned all the wisdom of the world
before even realizing
what had happened.

THE DREAMWALKER

From place to place
from city to city
from here to there
from there to here
I saw you passing quickly and devouring years
like a man whose house was burglared,
like a soldier crossing enemy trenches
on his motorcycle
carrying in his pocket a letter
to a general dead at the front,
like a film you once saw
where you bent your head on the chest of a mad girl
who was laughing hysterically
whenever she saw a dervish in a forest,
the devil closing in on him.
From there to here and from here to there,
I saw you chained in a castle
walled by high towers and barbed wire,
guarded by angels fresh from paradise,
in their eyes the drowsiness of barbarians,
while the ship, the only ship on the coast,
blew its horn for the last time
before it sailed you off to the frail waves,
roaring and raging—
distant islands and their houses, trees and their shade,
fickle seasons, coquettish seasons,
and someone you remember only to forget.
All of this is not a dream,
and it's not bad to remember it
because without it what would you have done
    with yourself?
Because without this how would you have seen yourself
    in the mirror?

This is what you used to call absolute forgetfulness
and it's nothing except an empty space.
From continent to continent
from planet to planet
falling down in a wave all the way to the bottom,
I heard the nymphs howling,
their heads poking out of the stone caves,
hiding among islands of reef
and flinging their poisoned kisses from afar.
I caught hope by her long hair,
clinging to her. I was drowning
and life was clawing my ribs
like a blood-crazed shark.
I was asleep on an island that resembled a city
I once saw in my dreams:
A treacherous monkey. Sinbad and the egg of a roch.
And that's the deep valley
where shepherds descend with ropes
to pick carnelian.
That's your howling I hear from a river bank obscured
        by fog,
your howling which you left there
on dry lips
for a man who always walks behind a cart
carrying lost souls
to paradise.
This howling is what you sing in exile
and no one hears you.
This howling is all you have down there in your well
as you listen to the wolf growl at the opening
waiting for your exit from the belly of the whale,
century after century,
like a trusted guard.
There's no refuge here. Hope is stupid.
A man breaks his promises, unrepentant in falsehood.
Still waters and a backyard. Where
is your sign, Mr. Policeman?

No, I will not persist in my requests.
Tomorrow I'll leave this prison on bail
and if that really happens
I'll make off with a submarine
and escape with it to the depths of the sea
with a boxer who used to stand on one foot
like the hand of the clock,
a singing parrot on his head.
There are no thieves here.
I only know a brigand
who used to slam the door behind him when he left.
There are always road blocks
and customs officers.
It's best that I go to a bar now
even if I'm broke.
The bartender knows me,
and they all know me
and what's more—
I have an eternal permit
to travel to hell.
In that city, everything is quiet at the front.
Don't be a hypocrite. A false sainthood under shades.
The situation wasn't all too well
because from the farthest points of the city
a man came striving for goodness
and I stood and gave him the military salute.
There's no difference in the end
and still I went to an empty theater
and gave a speech about history
crawling on its belly like a wounded soldier.
There were murdered people there,
always murdered people.
Thank God you weren't with them;
otherwise what would you have said
to the living among them?
This reminds me of a movie script
which I left behind in a temple.

All right, toss out the second scene
and from the first act throw out everything.
Nothing changes.
God's club is over everyone's head.
Let the atheists plot their conspiracies.
Let winter end.
Let the seasons pass.
There's always someone
waiting for you every night
in the city, in that city.

Never say goodbye.
Life is ahead of you
and one day,
inevitably,
you'll come
back to us.

GOOD MORNING, GOD!

Good morning, God!
I'm sure you know me well—
even though we never met before—
as you know all by name,
one by one,
the good ones and the bad.
I really wanted to visit you
to offer my loyal obedience,
but I didn't know your address in the sky
where there is a maze of stars and galaxies.
You know I'm not an astronaut
and I don't have a vehicle to carry me to you.
I know you're very busy;
we're all busy, to tell the truth, these days
even though I've been unemployed forever.
Still I ask you to please listen to me
as I tell you the opinions I have
on everything.
After all, you created me and threw me all alone
on this wretched planet.
I always heard a lot about you
even before I was born.
They all talk about you gravely
but with bad intentions.
I believe they intend to hurt you, sir.
They're all afraid of being shipped to hell
in closed crates,
or greedy for furnished apartments in heaven.
You know this better than I do, I'm sure.
That's really annoying, isn't it?
But why should this concern me
since I only wanted to talk to you as a friend
who's not concerned about gains or losses,
and since I want to talk to you

heart to heart,
as they say?

I thought of calling you
but I couldn't find your name
in the directory,
and so it'll make me very happy
if you'd call me
and try to lift my spirits
and ask me jokingly
"How are you doing, Fadhil,
in this ephemeral world?"
You know my phone number.
Call me any time you wish,
night or day.
I spend most of my time at home
reading, or writing, or watching TV,
and sometimes doze off
thinking about the fate of the world.
Really, let's meet once.
You too need some rest.
There's a lot I want to tell you,
a lot I haven't told anyone,
a lot I can't tell anyone but you.
And if you wish, I'll read you my latest poems
so that you'll tell me your opinion honestly.
And maybe we'd talk about the fate of humanity
or the fate of the universe
over a cup of coffee.
I have many plans and ideas.
I believe you'll like them.
I'd prefer we meet at my home,
and, at any rate, you know my address.
My name is written on the door.
All you'd need to do is ring the bell once
and you'll hear me calling from the hall:
The door is open. Welcome, God. Enter.
I have waited for you forever.

THOSE BEAUTIFUL DAYS

Don't lift the lid,
let the evil genie bemoan his bad luck.
Throw the bottle back into the sea.

Leave the forbidden fruit
on its tree in heaven
to be eaten by the silkworm,
and wait for the moth to leave its cocoon
and head toward the flame.

Let the chisel
become one with the stone.

Why do you care if the snake sheds its skin?
Your proof is the tree: deep through the wall
and in your sleep.

On the stone
the one emerging out of myths will stand.
Tell him to be kind to us.

If you reach the last oasis,
remember only your beautiful days.

We loved everything
to the end.

EXPLOSIONS

On this night and on every night
George Wetheril sits behind his telescope
watching the stars crash into each other
and explode, leaving their dust
in the labyrinth between galaxies.

On this night and on every night
a new star is born.
It too will be filled with inhabitants
and there will be a cave like the one
that belonged to the People of the Cave,
and monkeys on the trees flinging coconuts at us,
and cities like London, Paris, New York,
visited by tourists in summer.
And from time to time wars will break out
and at night husbands will sleep with wives
in the same beds,
above their heads, on the wall, the pictures
of their missing children.

In a thousand years . . .
in four million years . . .
in two hundred million years . . .

Dear George Wertheril,
let your telescope scope whatever it likes.
There's someone waiting for you out in the hall
claiming he is God.
He came to read you this poem.

ESCAPING, I REACH A RIVER

A fugitive from an impenetrable fort
armed by monsters who devour angels
from a camp glittering like a torn flag
where the desert's Bedouins light their fires in front of
      the closed gate
and release their barking dogs after me,
I meet the owl perched on its tree
and the clouds thundering, driven like armies at war.
I enter a valley through a maze of an impossible desire
and leave my traces on the rocks
for those coming after me.

Many temples I left for the conquerors,
and others I fenced with barbed wire
and shut their doors with red wax.

Escaping, I reach a river crossed by mules loaded
      with rifles,
led by thieves from mountains covered with snow
shelled by artillery from afar.
Cities lock their doors
and on the heads of their soldiers birds feed.

There, where a blind man wets his thumbs with his tongue
and counts his hidden dinars,
I turn over my many years
collecting them with tweezers from garbage dumps
like pearls to lace around the necks of ghosts,
knowing that memories are a savings account
in the fierce winter of old age
and that life
is what the eye sees after the first waking.

There, where there is no city at the end of the journey,
I raise a city leaning on its old castle
and walk with its derelicts returning at night from
      coffee shops
shooting their songs at the stars.

NAPOLEON'S HORSE

What do you know about the battle of Waterloo
except that a few soldiers in this trench or that
died for their country, as they say,
and that Napoleon was there on his red-brown horse
putting binoculars to his eyes
and following the battle?

I wish to stop this scene
as on a videotape,
to dress the wounded and bury the killed
and drive away the wolves coming from the hills
and enter a church and ring its bell to console the living
    forever.

At a circus in some city
I saw Napoleon's horse
led by a drunk clown with a whip.

THE KING AND HIS DONKEY

Once a donkey-tail grew on the king's back
and he cut it off,
and put it in a container
that he wrapped in cellophane
and tossed in the sea.
Once the donkey entered the king's palace
and brayed euphorically
and ran among the meadows.

Once the king sat
on a stone bench

and reflected on his days,
and his donkey's eyes
began to flood
with tears.

WHEN WE REACHED KAFKA'S HOUSE LATE

We left Prague behind us
and went up to the old castle
to look for a black house
inhabited by Franz Kafka.
—Mr. Kafka does not live here any more;
   maybe he moved to another city,
said the young man flirting with a girl on a stone bench.
A woman passed and whispered cautiously
—Please don't smoke in his presence;
   his health got worse yesterday.

On the road
we saw Gregor Samsa crawl out of his room
and hide behind a tree trunk.

And in the corridors that have no end
and the tunnels where rats live
there was a lit candle on a table.
Joseph K was there drawing his maps
as if he were a schoolboy.

We knocked on the door finally
and entered carrying flowers
thinking of what to say,
but we
arrived late as usual
and he was dead in his bed
staring out through the window.

PARTY

I'm thinking of having a party
attended only by the ones we love.
As for those who write their poems
regularly, we'll let them pursue their habit
in rooms with see-through mirrors
to be watched by everyone
or a few people at least.

What can be said will be said;
and, of course, what can't be said will be said too.
If we have to,
we'll pull the curtains and cover the windows.

And it will be my right,
since everything was arranged previously,
to make the camel
pass through the eye of the needle
with me on his back, of course.

THE LOST SON'S RETURN HOME

I got to walk that lonesome valley
I got to walk it alone
No one can walk it for me
I got to walk it all by myself
　　　　—from "Lonesome Valley," a gospel song

I open my eyes and see the sun through the curtain.
The rooster has returned to its coop
after it crowed three times on the wall
at the break of dawn.
There, the morning opens up over the roof
and descends the stairway, step by step.
Even the lone tree in the courtyard
is filled with anxious birds
landing in waves
from an open blue sky
that's like an overturned abyss.

There I heard the blind reciter
whose son was dragged into the army
recite the verses of the Quran
I learned by heart:
　　Have you not seen how your Lord
　　　　has dealt with the people of Ad,
　　The city of Iram with its lofty pillars,
　　The like of which none was created in the land,
　　And with the Thamud who cut huge rocks in the valley,
　　And with Pharaoh, lord of the stakes.
I lifted my head rising from sleep
like a child dreaming of heaven
surprised that I'm still alive.
All this light from the past!
All this noise in the city!
I open my eyes and fingers of light close them.
I think of a coachman whipping his two ragged horses
there in the dusty alley
where a cart stops in front of our house

41 AL-AZZAWI

and an old man gets out—his hands creased,
his eyes two cold holes—
returning from his distant exile
after a thousand years he spent lost in strange cities
begging ghosts for love
and his memories for repose.
On the stone stairway
I meet him
carrying the suitcase he bought
from a Jewish shop in Frankfurt.
Then he takes off his black sunglasses
and whisks me in his arms
taking me to wash my face near the well, mumbling
  Wohin des Wegs? Du stehst am Ufer Hier.
  Ich bin bereit, dich durch den Fluss zu tragen.
Look, there the cactus fruit has grown in the garden.
The sunflower plant is big again.
He lay there tossing his memories in front of me on
    the sand,
weeping over the child he once was.
  To see the World in a Grain of Sand
  And a Heaven in a Wild Flower,
  Hold Infinity in the palm of your hand
  And Eternity in an hour.
Ah, tell me who led you to the valley of ghosts?
What call led you to your fate?
Nothing except that I rose and saw a forest.
Nothing except that I saw a swarm of angels at dawn
going down into the valley, into the raised traps.
We caught many of them
and that was all,
believe me.

2) What have you gained from your bet, gambler?
standing by the oceans tossing your paper boats in,
waiting to arrive on another continent
to build a kingdom where the devil had been chased out
with sticks and brooms.

He flees to heaven leaving behind his victims
chewing on their memories.

What have you gained from your madness, mad one?
gripping your staff,
moving from one village to another
and from season to season,
crossing fires lit at night
by beggars who carry on their backs
bags filled with snakes.
What have you gained from your disobedience, disobedient
    one?
refusing to eat from the meat of sacrifices,
spilling your holy wine
in the gods' feast,
tossing pearls under people's feet,
digging with your shivering hand
your poisoned nail
into your own heart.
What have you gained from your wandering, poet?

3) In the broken mirrors a face steals a glimpse
of an age that has yet to come,
its arches hang in the air while the screaming soul of
    the prairie
wanders in tears, wearing her only mourning dress,
holding my hand, and pressing me with vampire teeth:
Never turn around.
Don't turn to the swallow left on the tree.
The charcoal sky nears our faces
like a dream that lives in the head, a dream a hunter
    plucks with a knife
and offers as bait to kind-hearted prostitutes
who walk at night on half-drunk streets
followed by children wearing pirates' clothes.
In every corner a mirror:
once I saw murderers standing at alley crossings
leaning on their rifles, sipping tea,

and finally the evicted workers came
from their caves, following a bus crowded with thieves.
This is not the right place to count mistakes.
There under the tree we can sit and deliberate
on the future of the world.
Have you ever seen a plane bomb a demonstration?
You can comfortably say that I was there
when the sky rained bombs.
I saw the pilot staring at us from his window.
I cursed him, but he paid me no mind.
His face remained stuck in my mirror
which I threw underfoot. The crowds walked over it
and it caught corpses from burned tanks
decorated with flags and posters.
In memory there is always a portrait of a quarrelsome devil
sticking out his tongue at me
sitting at his exquisite desk
under searchlights.

4) What markets have you passed by? How many women
have you met wrapped in their black robes crossing Old
Qaisaria toward your house followed by a young Kurdish
porter, his pushcart filled with pomegranates and oranges?
How many times have you climbed the fort? How many
times have you come down from the fort on the way to the
cinema to watch a film about Tarzan among the apes of the
jungle on your way to the café to meet friends who sit in the
evening and drink tea, talking about Gorky's mother or
Hemingway's fish. How many times have you crossed
Khassa Su River leaping over stones to reach a retreat on the
other side of the city and avoiding the spies on their
bicycles? How many times have you combed your hair and
oiled it? How many times have you parted it, hoping she'd
see you, the Turkoman girl you loved?
What cities have you left, what villages?
How many friends left you without saying goodbye?
How many wars broke out, in which you weren't killed?
How many jails have you entered?

How many poems have you written?
How many times have you walked down Rashid Street
and found yourself in a village on the German border?
And the trial they led you to in Basra,
how it turned into a café in Leipzig;
and the fat torturer in Al-Hilla Prison
why did he twine his thick moustache
while carrying his ropes on his shoulders?
And the clowns, why did they lead their monkeys
from the cane huts to the stone barracks?
And the grave diggers, how they placed their coffins
on carts pulled by donkeys
and slid from the orphaned hill
to the spring
to wash their hands from blood and dust before
    leaving again.

5) Each volition is a sign of fire.
Each fire is a sign of ash.
Each grain of ash a sign of stone with which the future
    is built.
Each future a sign of whatever rises now.
Whatever rises now is a sign of the cry that's never heard.
Each unheard cry is a sign of the one you cried before.

What belongs to Caesar will be yours alone.
The mountain will come willingly to talk to you.
Ah, don't tell him anything
as you must have secrets too.
Tell him you've waited a long time
and he'll understand.
This planet is the first stop
on the road to your home.

QUESTIONS

A man enters a mirror
and starts staring at me angrily.
—What crime have I committed?
A scream I hear
coming from all the ages.
Who released it?
A blind man plays a guitar
in an abandoned park.
Who heard him?
A child stands by the shore
and gives the sea my questions.

What do I do with the answers?

QUESTIONS AGAIN

A hand flung on a table,
there's ash in the hand.
What do I do with my hand?
What do I do with ash?

A child rises from sleep:
—Who woke me?
—Old age, son.

A dream falls to the ground
and bleeds.
—Does your wound pain you?

Someone is waiting.
Someone is waiting for someone else.
—Will he come?

A poet stands on a cliff
and screams.
—Do you hear his silence?

On the crosscurrent of the winds
I raise my kingdom.

THE PARTY

No one was missing.
Cain was in the kitchen sharpening his knife
and Noah in the living room watching
the weather report on television.

They all arrived in their cars
and disappeared in the long alley
leading to the party.

Our Fair Lady danced in the ring
and showed her treasures
through her transparent dress.
We sat with other guests
and sipped our drinks to the dregs.

At the end of the night,
returning home,
we gave the blind man his lost cane
and the murderer his bloody hatchet.

It was a party,
like any other party.

JOURNEY OF THE BANISHED

In a distant sky in the morning
they came in long lines
down to a deserted coast
and stood before fires
lit in old holes
and extolled strange deities
with mumbled prayers and raised hands
holding dead birds.
Baffled souls howl
like dogs in a city struck by a plague,
and a hawk with enormous stretched wings
glides over headless bodies.
Is this the end? I asked.
Or is it the beginning?
On that morning, on that fierce
cold morning,
they crossed
one passage after another
entering a desert
that opened its door to them
and disappeared.

Barbed wire. Stones and birds.
Bedouins. Prophets. Magicians and torturers
and someone weeping under a tree.
This morning is not my morning.
This child is not my son.

Over the oases blind birds flutter
and from the sky angels in the throes of death descend.
Deeply, deeply, we penetrated
with broken words on the mouths of the dead.
Far, far we rowed
with the stretched hands of the living.
Far we traveled on the roads of this planet.

Many cities we raided,
empty and dark cities.
Hollow bones in singing sands
and a black moon blossoming
like a lonesome flower.

In that refuge
seeing the last sign
on the mountain
where an old prophet, fires blazing
under his feet, talked to God,
I carried my solitude on my shoulder
in a bundle filled with sins
and rose up.

In some oasis
Bedouins disembarked.
They drank an old wine and slept
then woke in the last dawn
and listened to the four winds
storm eternity.
They rose quickly,
poked their crouched camels awake,
and walked on again.

SOLITUDE

A wave breaks on the rocks
leaving night on the coast
to listen to the genies' call
coming from the branches.

The moon split with the strike of an axe
sits hidden behind a stone, and falls slipping from my palm
onto the grass groaning in the valley.
Nothing here tempts me to build my kingdom,
nothing but the drone of days
as they roll down like balls
of ice.

THE COMPUTER'S EXHORTATION

A flat-nosed dog with a sausage. A dog devouring poems,
according to Carl Reinhardt's equations. What could I ask for
more? Poems, poems, poems wholesale, by poets whose talents
have dried up from lying too long in the tropical sun. Come
here, Baudelaire, and learn how to make wonder, where the
stork swallows a fish in the air and the computer squats in front
of me and composes its sad poems. A dictionary of poems on the
screen. Emotional formations and colorful gradations. All my life
I've been learning to form sentences and now this computer
comes fleeing IBM and starts producing poetry instead of me.
We quarreled. Professional envy. I told him "You don't know
how to write poems." He laughed, his cheeks puffed, and said
"Believe me I'm the greatest poet in the world. But why
jealousy? I'll write fantastic poems for you. Just put your name
under them or above, and publish. What else do you want?"
Then he started singing a new poem:

When darkness plays
the evening becomes a stone
Gold and beauty sometimes shine
I dance and I think
Usually grass excites me
The bell grows rude and golden
There in the bottom, mysterious roads and clerks
Who will give the plant a kiss?
The poet
Dreams and fish
Skinny and kindness
Blue appears the gazelle of dreams
A magical rhythm plays
and silence will rain tomorrow.

I think I'll show this poem to Al-Nabigha Al-Dhaibani. Your heritage is most important because it links you to your forgotten roots back to when you were an ape in the tree. I'm not an ape. I am a tree; in its branches a blind owl hides. Look for your grandfathers. Your heritage will guide you to them. Look for them—from Hatim Al-Taai who slaughtered his cattle for his guests to your uncle the Caliph Haroon Al-Rashid as he dreams of Zubaida walking naked to the pond. Throw Abu Nawas out of the Court. Ill-mannered Magus who serenades honorable Arab boys. Not all Persians are homosexual. I prefer Omar Khayam, a poet from Nisapur who was fond of young maidens and the blood of the vine. Did you read his last quatrain:

I was told the drunkard is damned
but that is not true, and can easily be disputed,
for if lovers and wine drinkers were in hell,
tomorrow paradise would be as empty as the palm
of a hand.

Not all Magi are evil. Three of them followed a star that led them to a cave inside a house in Bethlehem and they gave their gifts to Mary's child. Mary who shook the date palm fronds and sweet dates fell. Many generations ago our two armies met at Qadisiya and we fed them a painful torture. Sa'ad Ibn Abi Waqas dragged me by the hand and said I want you to lead the left flank, but I attacked from the right riding my piebald horse. Rustum, the Persian king, panicked and fell off his elephant, which he'd blindfolded with a rag, and fled to the rear. I chased him and felled him to the ground then dragged him by the feet all the way to Abu Gharaib Prison in Baghdad. He was a prisoner of war there for fourteen centuries. In the second Qadisiya we exchanged him with the CEO of the Rafadin Bank of Iraq in Arabstan. The man was jailed for issuing checks not covered by the balance of history. Then Hafiz of Shiraz came and read his poems in the Writers' Club in Al-Ulawiya.

> I said what are your lips.
> My lips are the water of life, he replied.
> I said what is your mouth.
> Ah, like the essence of all plants, he said.
> And what are your words, I asked.
> Hafiz, he answered, has called them
> prayer and the joy of every contented soul.

Thank God, Hafiz, Khudara shu, we're still friends despite everything. Let them kill each other. The generals to the dogs, and the leaders to hell. Let our motto now, and for all times, be "Poets of the World Unite!" We've become strong in the end. We will leave it to computers to cuss out our enemies. As for us, we'll recline on couches in our parlors, laughing at the lying sages and the idiotic leaders, and we'll tell each other stories of those who have passed.

LIFE WITH RATS

Crouched in darkness,
we ate from a pot placed on newspapers spread on the floor.
Rats jumped to snatch food out of our fingers
then stood in front of their burrows
readying for another attack.
On cold nights
they hid between our thighs
until we saw a giant rat in a forest
dragging behind him a weeping girl,
her neck tied with a rope.

In the morning, while we listened to the nightingale chirp
     in the tree,
we carried barrels of our urine
and dumped them in the ditch in front of the police station.
We came back with breakfast prepared for us by
     a policeman's wife
whom we'd made love to a thousand times in our dreams.

When evening came
they called us one after the other
and hung us from our shoulders to the ceiling fans
until rats began to fall
from the folds of our clothes
and howl from the whipping.

After a few years or maybe centuries
I saw the one I left in the darkness of the pit:
He was a young boy again wearing his pajamas as usual.
He lifted his head and stared at me for a long time
then went quickly on his way.
I think he has forgotten me in the throng of life.

THE APPLE

I remember I was lying in a garden when I saw Eve with her long black hair down on her shoulders shining in the sun that fell on her naked body. She rose and headed toward the forbidden tree and turned around to smile at me, encouraging. I was thinking of her supple body swaying in front of me. I felt like throwing her on the grass again, ignoring the parasitic angels watching us from the trees. They were taken by our daily coupling in heaven, so much that some began to take pictures of us secretly and hang them on their walls to stare at us morning and night. I stayed reclined in my place and Eve returned with the apple in her hand. I told her: Be reasonable and don't eat from the tree. There are spies watching us and they will take the news to God, for sure.

She shook her head dismissively, and biting
into the apple said:
Those unemployed indolents, let them die of envy.

I took the apple from her, and I too bit into it
despairing.

In that moment, in that exact moment I left non-being and saw the big bang: fireworks, lightning and storms, thunder and comets in the sky. No paradise and no angels. Holding Eve's hand I cried: Where to now, God? I did not hear an answer. The taste of the apple was still in my mouth. And as happens in dreams, we fell into a bottomless space toward some planet, a very distant planet. And I was happy.

Whenever a hand leans on the fence, the one ruined by soldiers coming from villages and distant cities on their way to their stone barracks, a slave stands by the castle's curtain and blows into a horn, and a hawk spreads its wings in the air and aims at my heart which I'd left in the prairie, beasts licking its blood as they left their dens.

Here between cities suspended in memory like lanterns at night, between dirt roads at noon trodden by tired caravans heading for a cave where thieves hid their treasures, I walk, the wind behind my shoulders, knowing that a man will meet me at the end of the journey or its beginning, and that I'll be his guest who will kill him one night and escape leaving my footsteps on the sand.

All these kingdoms, how do I enter them? All these stretched hands, how can I refuse them? All these wars, how can I lose them? All these rituals, how can I desecrate them?

Ah nothing except this arm which cannot reach, this severed arm behind a fence where dried grasses are piled in the sun, nothing except a pair of eyes watching soldiers with bayoneted rifles stabbing the wounded behind the trees.

And there on a grassy slope inhabited by birds and jackals I see astronauts landing their shuttles and leaving their gifts on the open road.

From behind the fence surrounding heaven I watch God with his roughened hands vexedly kneading Adam's clay, leaving it in the sun to dry. I dupe him and blow life into the statue and Adam rises to greet me embracing. "You are my son. I've been waiting for you." Fleeing, we cross mountains leaving God behind in his solitude making new statues.

There isn't a single star out this night. The longer we wait, the longer its absence extends. The moon in its waning and the wolf in the cave. Poisoned algae on the soul. And a coachman whips his horse in the morning. At the foot of the hill grasshoppers bounce about and plastic devils studded with rubies and jasper stroll public parks. There, finally, from the first caves the ape tribes come out, and we join them happily and descend toward the spring.

No matter how far,
my horse takes me.
In the end there is always
a cheap hotel awaiting us
and a stable full of hay.

THE FROG

In the prison hospital the doctor gave me a dose of Proloxin and I grew two legs like those of a frog. I was left alone in bed and my body was covered with sores. Nurses used to come by, and covering their noses with their hands, refused to dress my wounds. From my place here I used to see them inject the frogs with Inistin poison which is taken from curare, the chemical the Indians used to lace their poisoned arrows. Men were choking all the time and I heard their croaks coming from distant swamps. Men confessed their crimes on screens that broadcast live shows to us every night before we slept. There was weeping and grinding of teeth. Neurosurgery and gloves stained with blood. God keep the dead! the frog said as it leapt between the trees
returning to the torture chamber.

AFTERWORD

I encountered poetry at an early age. When I was fifteen I began publishing poems in the leading Arab literary magazines of Beirut and Baghdad, hiding from their editors the fact that I was still a schoolboy. And before that, at ten, I wrote my first poem imitating another poet who wrote in the ancient Arabic tradition. In those years I was immersed in reading the Arabic literary canon. Before discovering modern Arabic poetry as it was being launched from Iraq after the second world war, I was taken by the magical rhythms of the Quran, the loftiness of classical Arabic poetry, and the mythological tales of A Thousand and One Nights, along with other fantastic stories that one heard everywhere.

Now as I think of the distant past, I feel a great debt to the cultural diversity in my city Kirkuk; that varied exposure created the deepest impressions on my intellectual and poetic development. That city, located in Northern Iraq and known for its British-owned oil fields, and its inhabitants speaking Arabic, Turkish, Kurdish, and Assyrian (in addition to English, spoken by many who worked in the oil industry), gave me what I never received elsewhere: a sense of the play between poetry and life.

The Turkoman drunkards, as they, filled with euphoria, walked home from their taverns in the evening, some of them sang, in loud precise voices, quatrains called Khoryat, that they composed on the spur of the moment. As soon as one poet finished reciting his quatrain on love or the treachery of time, another voice rose from a nearby street with another quatrain in response to the first. A third or fourth voice might intervene continuing this poetic dialogue that took place between people who did not know each other. The poets forgot their nocturnal verses. But the people who heard these quatrains memorized the best of them and publicized them the following day without knowing their authors.

I did not write poetry then, but I knew that everything around me pulsated with poetry, an awareness that has helped me gather a tremendous store of memories, impressions, and sensations that still move me. One of my relatives, a dervish who wore his hair to the shoulders, took me frequently to the Sufi chant circles of dhikr (remembrance of God). The dervishes held these circles on Friday nights at their mosques in the Kurdish neighborhoods of Kirkuk. I crouched on the floor and stared in astonishment at men stabbing themselves with daggers without spilling a drop of blood, and men banging their hands on cymbals that were heated until they glowed red. At times I participated in these circles. One moved the head from side to side at first, then the rest of the body joined, repeating these motions seemingly endlessly until one reached a state called nashwa (ecstasy) whereby one lost awareness of all that surrounded him. In that moment, where all boundaries that separate the dervish from the universe disappear as if he is embarking on an endless journey in space, he reaches the magical intersection where the meaning of existence lies. In a way, this state, despite the different goals aimed at and the different means of reaching it, resembles Andre Breton's "moment of illumination" which he considered the essence of poetry. The insights I gained from participating in the Sufi circles led me to believe that poetry is not related to what is common and apparent in daily life except if it aims to reach an intense moment in one's being. The moment aimed at is that of complete revelation and exposure, despite all the unclarity that surrounds it, a moment of total meaning even if it seems meaningless within the sensual experiences of our bodies and souls.

If we are aiming high it is because we do not want to fall to the lowest rungs of human experience. In attempting to defend the victim's injured dignity, or at least in the name of that purpose, we have justified the worst forms of human behavior—everywhere and anywere wearing the blood-stained masks of torturers or dressing up in angel's robesIn my German exile, which has lasted for twenty years now, and before that in the three years I spent in the dictators' prisons, I discovered that poetry's power is akin to that of a saving fire which scares away the wolves that fill our age with their howling.

There is no poetry in a place uninhabited by people. We write to be read by others even though we are we fully aware that we live in a world filled with delusions peddled by diverse clergy who claim to know the way to paradise. These same lies are turned into commodities displayed in the marketplace—ideological goods, nationalist goods, religious goods. All of this is to control the people's souls and minds and to win their loyalty through the most base and barbaric means. One no longer needs to think since there is always someone thinking for him. Here is where I see the exceptional role of poetry: to confront the numerous lies and forgeries and to pull the masks off of the delusion-sellers' faces by affirming the truth that is buried under piles of commercialized and repetitive language, and to delve to the bottom of the deepest oceans to capture the jewels of speech. As poetry reminds us time after time of what is true in life, it also emphasizes knowledge over ignorance, civility and decency over barbarity, distinction over generalization, remembrance over amnesia, and more than anything, creativity over convention.

Unlike a clergyman or an ideologue who sees what he has always seen, a poet, because he has nothing but his own eyes, enters each city for the first time and can reflect life's raucous movements and penetrate inner depths where volcanoes explode and oceans rage. The poet, then, will disturb us, shock us, raise doubts in our hearts. And as he turns meanings around, as if magically, into visions and illuminations, he does do so not to prove a point like Christ treading water, but only to reveal a truth about life. In this way, too, the inner eye in each of us which is supposed to hold the deepest awareness of mankind's existential complexities begins through a poet's imagination to reshape everything in images colored in ways that cannot be seen outside poetry. Here comedy mingles with tragedy, play with seriousness, the dream with the real, the concrete with the intangible, and the meaningful with the meaningless.

Nietzsche once wrote "Inside each artist there is a child that wants to play." Before learning of this passage I had discovered the child-likeness of poetry, its innocence, and its ability to play through the voices of those unknown poets in Kirkuk. They taught me that a true poet plays on the side of the road for himself first and foremost, celebrating the world and, unconcerned about being recognized, revealing the secrets of his soul to others. Every true poet, in the end, is a singer on the side of the road. Today, as I write a new poem, I see that Turkoman poet returning home from the tavern, stumbling in front of me through an alley. He launches his poem in the night to rid his eyes of drowsiness and his heart of despair, and to forget the solitude of the road which he must walk alone.

QRL BACK ISSUES

— Original copies of the remaining file of scarce first editions, "perhaps one of the richest veins of original poetry, prose, and criticism in the literary landscape of the last half century."

THE 1940s

VOL. I, 4: _Poetry:_ Stefan George, O. Williams, Garrigue, J.G. Fletcher. _Prose:_ Brock, Heilman, Weiss $10
VOL. II, 4: _Poetry:_ cummings, Taggard, Moore. _Prose:_ J. T. Farrel, Kazin, Williams, Mizener, Snell $5
VOL. III, 3: Valéry Issue
2: _Poetry:_ Austin, Graham, Hardy, Hoskins, Stallman, Stevens $15
4: _Prose:_ Graham, Flores, Guerard,Weiss, Watts $10
VOL. IV, 2: Moore Issue $50
3, 4: _Poetry:_ cummings, Sitwell, Koch, Patchen, Schwartz, Rexroth, 12 Japanese poets, Eluard, Apollinaire, Williams. _Prose:_ Austin, Belitt, Bogan, Flaubert, Rexroth $10
VOL. V, 2: Pound Issue $5
1, 3, 4: _Poetry:_ Watkins, Simon, Cavalcanti, Eberhart, Gongora, Merrill, Shapiro, Villa, Wilbur. _Prose:_ Belitt, 3 Goodman plays, W. C. Williams, Zukofskynovella $15

THE 1950s

VOL. VI, 2: British Writers Issue. _Plays:_ Lawrence Durrell and Ronald Duncan. _Poetry:_ Campbell, Tomlinson, Ridler, Watkins, Nicholson $10
1, 3, 4: _Poetry:_ Carruth, Duncan, Gregor, Herbert, Lattimore, Lorca poems and essay, Merwin, Martial, Schubert, Triem, Walton, Williams. _Prose:_ Fiedler, Garrigue, Liben, Orlovitz $15
VOL. VII, 1, 2, 4: _Poetry:_ Casanueva, Cummings, 8 Dutch poets, Ford, Golffing, Heath-Stubbs, Mayhall, Olson, Seferis, Williams' Theocritus. _Prose:_ Elliott, Humphrey, Nakajima $30
VOL. VIII, 1: Leopardi Issue $5
2: _Poetry:_ Ashbery, Lattimore's Bacchylides, Hughes, Kessler, Fitts's Martial, Levin, Wright, Zukofsky. _Prose:_ Garrigue, Summers, J. Merrill play $5

VOL. IX,Rexroth's" Homestead Called Damascus" $5
4: _Poetry:_ Char, Dickey, Koch, Finkel Hughes, Merrill, Nathan, Nemerov, Morse, Pack, Rosenthal. _Prose:_ Rilke's letters to Supervielle $5

THE 1960s

VOL X,1-2: Hölderlin Issue $5
3,4: _Poetry:_ Cummings, Nathan, Dickey, Merrill, Seferis,Rudnik, Snodgrass. _Prose:_ Connors, Daniels, Ellison, Klabund $10
VOL. XI, 4: Montale Issue (on file only) $35
1, 2-3: Prize Award Issue: 2 plays by Holly Beye. _Poetry:_ Andrade, Fargue, Gregory's "Ovid," Hugo, Levertov, Jarrell's "Faust," Vliet, Wright. _Prose:_ Beye, Goodman play, Musil $40
VOL. XII, 1-2, 3: _Poetry:_ Bly, Eberhart Dickey, Duncan, Gregory, Hughes, Ignatow, Lieberman, Simpson, Sward, Rosenthal, Sullivan, Urdang. _Prose:_ Play by D. Finkel, 2 Chekhov stories, Jackson, Mellon, Ludwig, Gardner.$10
4: _Fiction:_ Cocteau's "Essay of Indirect Criticism" $5
VOL.XIII 20th Anniversary Double Issues, 1-2: _Poetry:_ Whitman, Hölderlin, Alberti, Ammons, Dickey, Gregor, Hecht, Jarrell, Jouve, Merrill, Levertov, Rosenthal, Shapiro, Stafford $10
3-4: _Fiction:_ H.D., Ellison, Humphrey, Brooke-Rose, Eich, Gardien, Leviant, Oates, Lattimore's Homer $5
VOL. XIV, 3-4: _Prose:_ Peter Weiss, Segal, Dostoevsky, Coover, Kleist $5
VOL. XV, 1-2: _Poetry:_ Brock, Char, Garrigue, Guthrie, Hugo, Montale, Seferis, Weiss, Kinsella, Ponge $10
3-4: _Prose:_ Borges, Coover, Friedman, Oates, Steele, Estrada, Kizer, Spacks $5

THE 1970s

VOL. XVI, 1-2: _Poetry:_ Amichai, Ammons, Belitt, Carruth, Coover, Duncan, Enzensberger, Essenin, Ghalib, Gregory, Guthrie, Hecht, Howard, Hughes, Levertov, Perse, Plath, Sexton, Seferis, Simpson, Rich, Wilbur $35
3-4: _Prose:_ Whitman, Coover, Ellison, Gonzalez, Merwin, Sartre $5

VOL. XVII, 1-2: _Poetry:_ Ponge, Merwin, Wright, Char, Davie, Eberhart, Kinnell, Pastan, Rakosi, Solzhenitsyn, Finkel, Gogol, Hecht, Holland, Kunze, Plumly, Swann $10
3-4: _Prose:_ Gardner, Busch, Eaton, Oates, Watkins $5
VOL. XVIII, 1-2: _Poetry:_ Cavafy, Celan, Mandelstam, Carruth, Dubie, Lieberman, Merwin, Milosz, Novalis, Peck, Ostriker, Sandy, Wright $10
3-4: _Prose:_ Mandelstam, Coover, W. Morris, Kleist-Brentano, Moss, Willard, $10

RETROSPECTIVE ANTHOLOGIES:

POETRY:

A discussion of open and closed verse by W.C. Williams, Richard Wilbur, and Louise Bogan; and poetry over the past three decades through the work of 146 poets including Stevens, Cavafy, Nemerov, Ashbery, Rich, Solzhenitsyn, Whitman, Dickey, Bishop, Merwin $25p

PROSE:

A Goodman play, a Zukofsky novella, diaries of Osip Mandelstam and Ben Belitt, stories, modern fables, translations by Ellison, H. D., Gardner, Humphrey, Coover, Morris, Borges, Garrigue, Merwin, Chekov $10p/15c

CRITICISM:

Cocteau on painting, Flaubert on Aesthetics, Dostoevsky on religion, Lorca on Gongora, Seferis on Eliot, Sartre on Mallarmé, Weiss on editing $10p/15c

SPECIAL ISSUES:

Combining 7 issues each dedicated to Pound, Moore, Kafka, Hölderlin, Montale, Valéry, and Leopardi, with articles on the writers and new poetry, stories, or translations by Williams, Stevens, Bishop, Ransom, Bogan,Brooks, Rilke, Lowell; Eliot, Merrill, Heidegger $10p/15c

POETRY SERIES:

Publishing 4 to 6 prize-winning books in one volume: 1978 —

VOLUME XX: *Burrows's* "Properties: A Play for Voices," based on the diaries of Fanny Kemble, actress, abolitionist, feminist; important first poetry books by *Brian Swann* ("Living Time"); *Reginald Gibbons* ("Roofs, Voices, Roads"); *M. Slotznick* ("Industrial Stuff"); and *David Galler's* "Third Poems, 1965-1978) $10p/15c

VOLUME XXI: *Jane Flanders'* "Leaving and Coming Back"; *Jeanne Foster's* "A Blessing of Safe Travel"; and *John Morgan's* first book, "The Bone-Duster"; Canadian *Anne Hébert* tr. by *Poulin;* a play by *Sidney Sulkin* "Gate of the Lions." $10p/15c

VOLUME XXII: debuts by *Mairi MacInnes* : "Herring, Oatmeal, Milk and Salt"; *David Barton's* "Surviving the Cold" called possibly this year's most distinguished" in *Hudson Review;* *Phyllis Thompson's* third book, "What the Land Gave"; Brazilian poet *Carlos Nejar* tr. by *Piccioto;* and Korean poet *So Chongju* tr. by *McCann* $10p/15c

VOLUME XXIII: *Jane Hirshfield's* lyrical first book, "Alaya"; *Marguerite Bouvard's* "Journeys over Water"; *Christopher Bursk's* evocations of the perilous adventures of childhood, "Little Harbor"; one of Poland's most splendid poets, and 1996 Nobel Prize winner *Wislawa Szymborska,* tr. by *S. Olds, Drebik,* and *Flint;* and Swedish poet *Lars Gustafsson* tr. by Gustafsson with Australian poet *Philip Martin* $20p/25c

VOLUME XXIV: *David Schubert: Works and Days.* Celebrates the poignant poetry of "one of America's best poets" (Ashbery). All of Schubert's mature poems are presented; in addition, a biography, composed of early poems and letters, with other's memoirs and letters, dramatically recreates this poet of the '40s. "A remarkable document: haunting, sus-penseful, original, deeply moving" (Oates) Essays on Schubert by Ashbery, Ehrenpreis, Ignatow, Wright $10p/15c

VOLUME XXV: *R. Denney's* poem on architecture, "The Portfolio of Benjamin Latrobe"; translations by *Swann* and *Scheer* of eminent Spanish poet *Rafael Alberti's* "Rome: Danger to Pedestrians"; *Nancy Esposito's* powerful first book, "Changing Hands"; *Larry Kramer's* unwavering exploration of family, "Strong Winds Below the Canyons"; and a poetic foray into a den of deconstruction, "Canicula di Anna", by *Anne Carson*$15c

VOLUME XXVI: *James Bertolino's* third volume, "First Credo"; "The Diver"; by *Warren Carrier; Frederick Feirstein's* explorations of rowdy origins in "Family History"; vivid first books by *Julia Mishkin* ("Cruel Duet") and *Joseph Powell* ("Counting the Change") and Bulgarian *Nicolai Kantchev* tr. by Kessler and Shurbanov $15c

VOLUME XXVII: "Sky in Narrow Streets" from distinguished Welsh poet and doctor *Dannie Abse;* the premier Portuguese poet *Eugenio de Andrade's* "White on White" tr. by *Levitin; Joan Aleshire's* "This Far", a celebration of the possibilities and limits of language; *David Keller's* skillful first book, "A New Room"; and *Peter Stambler's* dramatic sequence on the Schumann family, "Unsettled Accounts" $35c

VOLUME XXVIII-XXIX: QRL's 45th anniversary includes *Reg Saner's* "Red Letters", lucid meditations on the rocky vastness of Colorado; *Jeanne McGahey's* remarkable "Homecoming with Reflections" (one of *Voice Literary Supplement's* "Best books of the year"); *Jarold Ramsey's* "Hand-Shadows", an unflinching journey through the wilderness of human relationships; and Australian *Craig Powell's* brave, trenchant work, "The Ocean Remembers it is Visible" $10p/15c

VOLUME XXX: *Jean Nordhaus's* graceful poetry of knowledge, "My Life in Hiding"; *Bruce Bond's* "The Anteroom of Paradise", explorations of composers and painters; *Geraldine C. Little's* absorbing "Women: In the Mask and Beyond"; *B. H. Fairchild's* powerful poems of the everyday, "Local Knowledge"; and *Judith Kroll's* "Our Elephant and that Child" persuasive treatments of Indian realities and mysteries $15c

VOLUME XXXI: *Jeanne Murray Walker's* "Stranger than Fiction"; Israeli poet *Dan Pagis,* who "tempers outrage at absurdity with sad, knowing wit" (*Library Journal*) in "Last Poems", tr. by *Keller;* *Anita Barrows'* The Road Past the View"; Uruguayan *Cristina Peri Rossi's* "Babel bárbara" tr. by *Decker;* *Naomi Clark's* expansive "The Single Eye"; and distinguished French poet *Yves Bonnefoy's* "Beginning and End of Snow" tr. by *Sapinkopf* $10p/15c

VOLUME XXXII-XXXIII: 50TH ANNIVERSARY ANTHOLOGY: new poems by all the poets in the Poetry Book Series, including 10 new poems by Nobel Laureate W. Szymborska, plus poems from most of QRL's important poets out of its first 30 years.   20p/25c

VOLUME XXXIV: *Suzanne Paola's* confident first book "Glass"; *Frederick Feirstein's* poetic sequence "Ending the Twentieth Century"; Swedish poet *Werner Aspenstrom's* "Selcted Poems," translated by *Robin Fulton;* *James Bertolino's* "Snail River"; and *Paula Blue Spruce's* poetic play about Native Americans, "Katsina".   10p/15c

VOLUME XXXV: Lynne Knight's first full-length collection, "Dissolving Borders"; Jean Hollander's lightfooted "Moondog"; David Citino's blend of the lyric and dramatic, "The Weight of the Heart"; Barbara D. Holender's wily "Is this the Way to Athens"; and Romania's leading woman poet, Maria Banus, with her first book translated in the United States, "Across Bucharest After Rain". 10/20

QRL
26 Haslet Ave.
Princeton, NJ 08540

Edwards Films Presents...

LIVING POETRY

With The Poet
THEODORE WEISS

TWO UNIQUE FILMS

follow the evolution of a poem across time and through the process of revision.

Living Poetry: A Year in the Life of a Poem *(a Blue Ribbon winner at the American Film and Video Festival)*

The fimmaker, Harvey Edwards, filmed the creation and evolution of a poem by Theodore Weiss, "Fractions," from the initial inspiration to the finished product: a year's work—writing, revising, re-living the past and incorporating the present.

Living Poetry 2: Yes, with Lemon *(Bronze Plaque Award from International Film Council)*

Later, Edwards learned that Weiss had re-written the "final" version. He returned to make a new movie with a different approach: a group of Princeton undergraduates, led by their professor, James Richardson, discuss this final version of "Fractions."

The new "Fractions" still contains the lyrical elements that distinguish the first film, but the canvas has been enlarged: from the depths of the past, Weiss plumbs the terrible moments of growing up. Fires flash through the film—the memory of his house burning as a child sends the poet's imagination toward the larger fires of the world. At the same time a cup of tea and the kneading of bread in a warm kitchen become metaphors out of the daily for what, even in the face of catastrophe, remains.

The Final version of "Fractions" also appears in Theodore Weiss's latest volume of poetry, *A Sum of Destructions* (Louisiana State University Press).

These are films on the creative process and the importance of revision. Meant for schools, libraries, and the general public, they are tools to help people understand the creative workings of the thinking mind.

Theodore Weiss has taught at the Univeristy of North Carolina, Yale University, Bard College, and Princeton University. He has been poet-in-residence at M.I.T., Washington University, Monash University in Australia, Beijing University in China, and, for two years, a guest at the Institute for Advanced Study. He has published fourteen books of poetry, several books of criticism and many articles. He and his wife have published and edited *The Quarterly Review of Literature* for more than fifty years.

Edwards Films & Videos
Rentals & Sales
Center Road, RD1, Box 290
Eagle Bridge, NY 12057